Shepherding the Seasons

SHEPHERDING THE SEASONS

Stories from a Life with Two Flocks

CATHERINE FOOTE

the pilgrim press

since 1640

May you always know the care of a Good Shepherd

Cath Foote

The Pilgrim Press, 700 Prospect Avenue East
Cleveland, Ohio 44115-1100
thepilgrimpress.com

Interior artwork by Rebecca Rickabaugh, an artist and illustrator who lives on Whidbey Island. She is also a member of Catherine Foote's Seattle flock.

Printed in the United States on acid-free paper.

20   21   22   23   5   4   3   2   1

Cataloging-in-Publication Data can be found online at the Library of Congress. ISBN 978-0-8298-2108-6

∽

Dedication

∽

For my Seattle flock:
everyone who is part
of the faith community of
University Congregational
United Church of Christ in
Seattle, Washington;

and for Chris,
who has been there
since the beginning.

CONTENTS

∞

INTRODUCTION

I AM CALLED to be a shepherd of two flocks. "Call" is a spiritual concept of vocation that denotes both mystery and certainty. It was improbable that I should be a shepherd of any flock. I did not grow up on a farm, yet I now raise sheep in northwest Washington, on Whidbey Island. Though I was not raised in a church, I now serve as pastor to a large congregation in Seattle.

"Pastor" is Latin for "shepherd" and evokes for me images of care, enthusiasm, and diligence. Jesus called Peter to be a shepherd, and the Apostle Paul used the same term for himself and other church leaders. Stylized shepherd's crooks are featured in the garments of popes and bishops. When I became a pastor more than twenty-five years ago in California, shepherd imagery from scripture shaped my understanding of call. Still, "shepherding" remained a metaphor through the years. Then I finally got an actual flock of my own.

I became an actual shepherd almost twenty years ago, in Oregon. Growing up as a city girl, my exposure to farm life was limited to romantic images from books and movies, and trips to the county fair. When I went to the fair, I always walked past the rides and games and headed straight for the animal barns, first to see the horses, and next, always, to see the sheep. I knew nothing about those wooly creatures, but they drew me in. When, as an adult, I moved to Northern California and pastored a congregation there, I got a border collie. The border collie eventually, inevitably, led me to a farm and to sheep. I now raise Romneys, a wool breed that originated in southern England and was imported to the Pacific Northwest about one hundred years ago.

In balancing my life between two flocks, I draw my spirituality and my sense of the sacred from both. My Whidbey flock keeps me grounded. My Seattle flock keeps me engaged. Both flocks keep me busy.

Once, after the end of a particularly exhausting day of dealing with the needs of my Romney flock, I posted a question on Facebook: "Remind me again why I keep sheep."

I had just unloaded two tons of eastern Oregon grass hay, which I had hauled on a trailer, in the rain, up to my little farm on Whidbey Island, in western Washington. The trip had already been six hours before I caught a ferry for a twenty-minute ride across the waters of Puget Sound. When I pulled up my driveway, it was well after dark. I decided to do chores before I heated some leftover soup for dinner. I moved the sheep into the barn and fed the dogs. Then I unloaded the hay before it got any wetter, stacking it carefully with the wettest hay where I could feed it first. Halfway through unloading, the power went out, and I had no lights in the barn.

Just before midnight, I finished my work and headed to the house. I was wet and tired and cold. The house was dark. I still had not had dinner. The next morning, I would be getting up before daylight to turn the sheep out into the field and feed the dogs, before catching the early morning ferry into Seattle to get to church. I used the last of my energy to post my Facebook question and then crawled into bed.

The next morning the power was still out. I dressed in the dark, did my morning chores, and hurried to the ferry. I passed a power company repair crew working on lines downed by a large tree that had fallen halfway across the road. "It's going to be a while," I thought. Then, on the ferry, I checked Facebook to see if anyone had responded to my flippant post.

There was a note from my colleague Amy, who had apparently been up at midnight too. She sent a picture of her young son Benjamin on the farm when he was much smaller, with the note, "To remind you of better times." In the picture, the sun was shining, the grass was green, and Benjamin was clearly enjoying himself. I smiled. It did, indeed, remind me of that wonderful connection between my two flocks.

My sister answered the question, "To have something to do in your spare time." Right. A friend posted, "They give you lots of stories to tell." Yes. Another friend commented, "Because you love it." Thank you. "Otherwise, what would you do for fun?" said someone I have known since I was in eighth grade. A congregant compared my two flocks. "Because they're easier to deal with than people?"

One by one, my friends and family, my congregation and my community reminded me of what I needed to remember: these are the ways I stay grounded in all the sacredness of creation. From across the ocean, my friend Jane had written, "Because you like Welsh sheep shearers?" "Eifion told me to write that, by the way," she added.

The most moving comments came from folks who took my question much more seriously than I did. "It's your calling," said one person from my congregation. Another friend posted, "You are a pastoral shepherd, they are pastoral sheep. They go together."

The whole thing was summed up succinctly and wonderfully by my friend Brian, who was helping me train my dogs. He had not known me long at all, but he had seen my sheep run over me and my dogs ignore me, so he knew me well enough. He commented, "Because you are a Shepherd." He even capitalized the "S."

By the time I crossed the Sound to Seattle that morning, I had been reminded not only of why I do what I do, but of who I am. As a pastor, I tend the souls of people in their times of deepest need. I challenge people to be faithful to their deepest beliefs. With my congregants, I notice all the ways the Holy shows up in the world.

Then, at the end of the day, I go home to my other flock and a different set of chores. My sheep on Whidbey keep me grounded, and my tending of this flock is spiritual too. I am nurtured by the pattern of rising early to my tasks, by the day-in and day-out demands of the animals, without regard to season or weather, by the sheer physicality of moving tons of hay from truck to barn to feeder, by the quiet evenings watching over the flock as they graze their way back down to the barn. For almost two decades now, the farm has been my classroom and the sheep and the other animals there have been my patient, persistent instructors. Just when I think I have mastered my lessons, I find myself humbled by some new humorous or hard reality. I sense that if I can just notice what is around me, if I can be aware of this ordinary moment, of the animals in my care, of the ground on which I stand, my spirit will be fed.

This book is a collection of stories of my two flocks, through the course of the year. In these stories are the rhythm of the seasons, the tasks I return to again and again, the delight and the challenge of shepherding those flocks, and the deep spirituality of grounded living. They are offered to others who are shepherds, or sheep, or both, as we all are care givers and the ones cared for in one way or another. These stories are offered to those who recognize themselves as pilgrims carrying their own blessed stories on a journey to their own sacred practices and places.

Church Time

ADVENT

———◆———

———◆———

Farm Time

DECEMBER

IN THE BLEAK MIDWINTER

It is not quite 5 AM on Sunday morning. I am up early to tend both of my flocks, getting farm chores done before catching the ferry into Seattle to lead worship. The air is cold, the ground is frosty, and I can see my breath as I carry hay from the barn to the pasture. The sheep are still bedded down, but they have taken note of my activity and are beginning to stir. They know that breakfast comes before dawn on Sundays. In the sky a sliver of moon accentuates the dark. I stop for a moment and look up toward my house. On such a dark morning, I find comfort in the warm glow of light through the windows.

This Sunday morning, there is something more. In addition to the interior lights, strings of brightly colored lights run across the roofline and outline the porch. I display Christmas lights every December, even though from the road they can barely be seen. My animals and I are the ones who have a chance to really enjoy them. And on this cold, dark morning they are having their effect. They are reminding me that Advent has begun.

The liturgical season of Advent marks the beginning of the church year and the anticipation of Christmas. Advent always commences on a Sunday, known in many churches as the Sunday of hope, which is followed by the Sundays of peace, joy, and love.

Advent has a Latin root meaning "coming." The church world uses the word to indicate an expectant waiting for the arrival of the Christ child. In today's commercial world of Christmas decorations up before Halloween, it is hard to hold Advent as a season of waiting for Christmas. Even though we may have heard "Joy to the World" pumped through shopping malls all of October and November, it still seems strange to sing it in church before the day we actually celebrate the birth. However, it is hard to wait. At my church, people start asking for the Christmas carols at the beginning of December.

On the farm, by Advent I have moved into a long season of rain and snow and ice that challenges even the most enthusiastic ruralist. Morning chores are dark and cold. When the ground freezes, walking to the barn is like walking across a choppy ocean of mud that has turned miraculously solid. I wonder if the water Jesus is said to have walked on felt as sharp against his sandals as the frozen edges of mud feel against my boots. As the account goes, he too was walking in the darkness, and no doubt the storm had made the Sea of Galilee as rough as any frozen mud-ocean.

The sheep seem to prefer their mud frozen, as they easily crunch their way across it from the barn to the pasture in the morning. Freezing temperatures, however, also mean ice in the water buckets, until the good shepherd hauls hot water from the house to melt it. The metal waterer set out for the chickens freezes too. I run hot water on it to get it open so my hens can drink. It will freeze again each night the temperature drops, and I will repeat the ritual every morning.

Several years back, the temperature dropped to 17 degrees over Thanksgiving weekend, and everything froze. Because I was away from the farm celebrating the holiday with my family, I wasn't there to keep the warm air (such as it was) circulating through the house. A pipe in my bathroom was among the "everything" that froze. Then it broke. Then it thawed out. On Thanksgiving morning, the friend who watches my animals while I am away discovered water flooding my bathroom, laundry room, and kitchen. I took it in stride, as a part of what it means to live on a farm. Of course, houses in the city had frozen and broken pipes too. Winter is the time of year when everything is stripped bare—whether by frozen pipe or waning light—and we discover what is worth hanging on to, and what we have to release. In winter, the landscape is stark, and one can see great distances. Yet most of what is happening is unseen. The seeds planted in the fall lie underground, beneath the mud or snow or ice, holding on to their precious potential until spring. The tiny lamb embryos are growing inside the ewes.

The year of the house flood, I saw my kitchen floor stripped of the actual flooring so that only the subflooring was there. I could see where the original 1920s house ended. The tongue and groove subfloor gave way to the plywood used in the 1990s addition. I could see the decisions that were made by people who were in this house before me. Most of those decisions were pretty good ones. I dream about decisions that are now mine to make, as I work to be as faithful as those who came before me in my choices about what I will renew, what I will replace, and what I will let go. I like to imagine those coming after me might say that that those decisions were good ones too.

WHAT THE ANIMALS KNOW

It is no coincidence that the northern hemisphere arrives at the winter solstice right in the middle of Advent. In the middle of the fourth century, church leaders decided this was the ideal time to anticipate the birth of Jesus. Christmas is coming.

However, even before there was a Christmas, human beings knew the rhythm of the planet. The solstice was noticed and marked with celebration. Before the Roman emperor Constantine celebrated a December 25th Christmas in 336 AD, the Romans celebrated the solstice as *Dies Natalis Solis Invicti,* "the birthday of the unconquered sun."

In Seattle, my congregation looks forward to this solstice time in our particular Christmas way, with the proclamation of good news to all and peace on earth, with shepherds watching flocks and magi traveling from the east to honor a newborn king. We offer three worship services on Christmas Eve, including a pageant where everyone who wants to play a role is given one, just by showing up.

One year, just a day before the solstice, when the ground was hard and the sky still an inky black as I headed out for my morning chores, I found myself wondering whether or not the sheep knew what I knew—that after that day, our planet would begin its almost imperceptible turn back toward the sun. After all, the sheep don't seem to mind turning out in the darkness and have no trouble finding their way to the feed trough even when I have to carry a flashlight to be sure I don't trip on my way from the house to the barn. Do they look forward to the return of longer days?

Does my rooster, who crows not only at dawn but any time he feels like it, know when dawn will begin greeting him earlier and earlier?

Do my dogs, who rise faithfully when I do and accompany me every morning without even seeming to notice when it is still dark outside, anticipate the return of morning light as much as I do, and the time when even our earliest chores will be lit by the sunrise?

The answer, I've decided, is "Yes." If there is one lesson I continue to learn on my farm, it is to trust the wisdom of my animals. It's a lesson I have not mastered, but I know there is deep wisdom all around me in this place. I have sent my dog out to the far field to find a lost sheep, telling her "No" every time she returned to the barn, only, finally, to find the missing sheep right there, under the barn, where she had been all the time. My dog knew.

I have argued with the ewe who insisted on staying out in the field after giving birth to a lovely lamb, while I was trying to usher her to safety and warmth. "Why won't she just follow me?" I asked myself, frustrated. Then she had her second lamb, the one I did not know was coming. After the second birth, she quite willingly followed me with both her babies back to the barn. The sheep knew.

I have railed against people who would call sheep, or chickens, or any animals "stupid," countering that they just have a wisdom that fits them, and one we would be wise to pay attention to. Then I ignore my own advice.

The return of the sun and the lengthening of days will not be felt immediately. January and February will still be cold, even colder than December. The long nights will continue to be dark, and in the country the darkness is very deep. Most of the time I appreciate the darkness, but when the power goes out during a storm and I'm trying to find a black sheep who took a left turn at the barn door and headed for the pasture, it's a challenge. In our human world, it can feel like the darkness is everywhere. It can seem as if the light will never reappear. However, solstice observations and Christmas celebrations and even my daily farm chores serve to remind me that the return of light is inevitable. We wait, faithful to the

Advent season, with certain expectation. We humans are just one part of the rhythm of the world. My own animal self, buried beneath layers of civilization, knows this. So I will still rise, even in the dark, to do my winter chores.

AWAY IN A MANGER

Many years ago at our congregation's Advent workshop, we made four mangers. The project was offered with the "more active" children in mind; we thought working with wood and nails would keep them occupied. As the official manger expert, I drew up a pattern, purchased the materials, cut the wood into the correct lengths, and wrote out careful instructions about how to assemble the parts. Bob, one of our congregation's resident woodworkers, brought a selection of hand tools and supervised the construction.

We were right about the active children. They enjoyed the work of fitting and drilling and fastening wood to wood. By the time we were done, we had four nifty little mangers constructed by many proud builders. I was pleased with how they turned out.

Three of the four mangers went to my farm, where they are used regularly. They generally stay in the barn to hold the grain or apples that entice the sheep in at night. In the spring, when I set up the lambing jugs—the small pens where new-born lambs spend their first few days of life bonding with their moms—I put one of the mangers in each pen. The little feeders are just the right size to hold the nutrient-rich alfalfa for ewes to eat as they feed their babies. The three mangers in my barn are now well-worn. They are dirty and wobbly and have been repaired many times over the years.

The fourth manger the children built at that workshop remained at church. It has been used repeatedly as the manger for our annual Christmas pageant, with fresh straw every year to prop up baby Jesus. I usually don't pay much attention to it, but a few years ago, when we were all practicing our pageant parts just before Christmas Eve, I had a chance to see it again close up. The manger at the church is still clean and sturdy. There are no hygienic concerns when children gather around it every Christmas. If Joseph and Mary place their infant there during the pageant, it holds up without a problem. But my barn mangers? Uh, no.

I love all four of the mangers those children built more than a decade ago. They are useful tools for both of my flocks. They each hold deep memories of love and nurture and care.

In the closet where we store the pageant supplies, including the church manger, there are also several shepherd's staffs. Some are made of plastic, and some are bamboo. They are fine for the pageant; none of them, though, would be of any use on the farm. For a shepherd, a good working staff can be critical.

One March, while we were shearing sheep, I lost my most useful shepherd's staff. I was using it out in the ram pen while trying to catch a particularly wily guy and in the process fell backward into the mud. Filthy as I was from that adventure, I was proud to have caught him. He was the last sheep we had to shear, after which I went up to the house and took a long shower. By the time I went back for my staff, it was nowhere to be found. I figured someone had picked it up and put it in the barn, or perhaps the disgruntled ram had hidden it. In any case, I thought it would show up. It didn't.

My search for the shepherd's staff was unsuccessful through the spring and summer; without it, I caught all my lambs by hand. Then, about a month before Christmas, I found the lost staff. The grass around the fence had finally died back, and there it was. The wood shaft was warped and cracked, but the strong metal hook was fine. Once I repaired it, the staff became a useful shepherd's tool again.

There could not be more of a contrast between that hard-working shepherd's staff and the shepherd's crook I brought home from a trip to Scotland. I visited the craft tent at every sheepdog trial I attended, looking for just the right staff. I finally found the one I wanted at the International Trial in Tain, in the Scottish highlands. The crook was handmade by a "stickmaker" from the Isle of Harris in the Outer Hebrides, who told me as I admired his work that he had once made a crook for Prince Charles. The shaft is a lovely polished hickory, and the hook is from the horn of a Jacob's ram.

For all its beauty and grace, the shepherd's crook from Scotland is "for decorative purposes only." It can be a nice walking stick. It looks lovely in my office at church. I could even walk to the handler's post with it in a sheepdog trial. But this crook will never be used in a mucky pen to snag a sheep that is trying to dodge its haircut. If I tried to use it for that task, the stick and I would lose and the ram would win.

I love my Christmas decorations. Every year I set out my lovely porcelain shepherds and pristine sheep on the piano. In my crèche, Joseph carries a fragile little staff. However, the shepherds abiding in the field according to the Gospel of Luke were surely the muddy kind of shepherd, with the useful, battered staffs. The little Lord Jesus likely lay down his sweet head in a well-worn manger that had been overturned into the mud more than once. Luke's image is profound. In today's terms, the Gospel might have said Jesus was born in the car that had become his family's home when they lost their apartment. Or maybe Luke would tell us the baby was born in the tent city that took his parents in when they showed up in town with no place to stay.

My barn mangers and my well-used shepherd's staff remind me that the stories of Christmas are not intended for decorative purposes only. Living out the deepest meaning of this season might mean I get a little less decorative and a little more useful. To experience "God with us," we might pay attention to the messy mangers in the barn as well as the clean, sturdy manger in the annual Christmas pageant. As the story goes, it could be anywhere that we see God face to face.

THE FRIENDLY BEASTS

There aren't many Bible stories that feature animals. Noah's ark, of course. The talking donkey, a fascinating story found in Numbers 22. The Bible is mostly stories about people.

The birth narratives of Jesus are no different. In spite of Christmas carols, cards, and legends, only sheep are actually mentioned in the Bible stories of Jesus' birth, and they are simply in the region, being watched over at night.

Mary and Joseph travel from Galilee to Bethlehem; maybe a donkey carries them. The baby is born in a stable; maybe there are cows. Angels appear to shepherds; maybe the shepherds take some sheep along with them to see the baby lying in a manger (although anyone who has ever tended sheep will tell you it would be a big mistake). At least one of our church's Christmas picture books includes a border collie arriving at the stable with the shepherds—an absolute necessity, in my opinion, if you are going to bring a bunch of sheep to a birth. It had better be a very good border collie at that. Matthew's Gospel features magi from the east bearing gifts; maybe camels come with them.

Every crèche I've ever had features animals. When I was little, it was the animals that drew me to the scene. In fact, this is still true. If there aren't animals around, the nativity scene isn't that interesting to me. Before I cared for sheep of my own, I imagined those crèche animals pretty much as they appear in porcelain: gathered around, posed reverently, and standing still. It is comforting to imagine the infant Jesus being surrounded by friendly beasts. The reality of it all, of course, is very different. I can't imagine bringing lambs anywhere if I am in a hurry to get there.

The animals gathered around the mangers in our crèches and the animals in our lives remind us of our connection with all of creation. We recognize the vulnerability we all share. Those animals evoke tenderness in their reminder that—no matter how messy our Christmas or our lives might be—God is with us in the mess.

The animals free our imagination as well. The Christmas carol "The Friendly Beasts" is based on the legend that at the stroke of midnight on Christmas Eve, just as Christmas Day begins, animals can talk. In Greek, Aramaic, English, or the tongues of Pentecost, they greet one another and speak.

Thus every beast, by some good spell,
in a stable dark was glad to tell
of the gift she gave Emmanuel,
the gift she gave Emmanuel.

According to the animal legend, if you are in the right place at the right time, you might hear the animals speaking, praising God, laughing together in joy in the first moments of Christmas Day. In some countries it is said that children sneak off to stables to listen for the sound.

On Christmas Eve, our church has a candlelight service of lessons and carols that ends at midnight. Back on the farm, my sheep are already in the barn, settled down for the night. Because I am in Seattle and they are on Whidbey Island, I have never been there to test the legend of talking sheep as Christmas Day begins. But no matter. I have been listening to the sheep all year. And they do, indeed, say, "Praise."

REAL CHRISTMAS EVE

Life as a shepherd has caused me to read the stories of Jesus' birth differently. The Gospel of Luke says that Jesus was born in a stable, because there was no room for his pregnant mother in Bethlehem's inn. I once helped my veterinarian do a caesarean delivery of a lamb in my barn. I had called him at 3 AM when it was clear my ewe was in more trouble than she and I could sort out on our own. I was surprised by the lengths to which the vet went to create some kind of sterile environment right in the middle of the muck. There he was, carefully donning gloves, unwrapping packets of instruments, responding to possible contamination as if he was in a pristine operating room. The lamb was not alive when we got to it, but with good antibiotics, the ewe survived that surgery. I picture Mary having her first child in a stable and I shudder. I imagine Luke intended us to shudder. Jesus comes to us in the most humble of forms.

The shepherds, too, were out in the field watching and listening. It is at night that any shepherd is listening most carefully. Night is when the predators come. These shepherds, though, did not hear wolves, but angels. Still they had to be told, "Be not afraid."

It is interesting to be a shepherd at Christmas time. Every year I listen to the marvelous carol "Rise Up, Shepherd, and Follow," which mixes Matthew's star (which the magi rose up and followed) and Luke's shepherds (who were sent to a manger by angels). Even with the mixed-up stories, though, I like the carol. I like Luke's shepherds too.

Shepherding is humble work. One year I was walking through the pool of mud that our Washington winter rains create right in front of my barn. As I turned to close the door, my heel caught on a board. My foot was held tight, but my body was still moving. Down I went, on my back, sinking into the muddy pool about three inches before I hit anything solid. I lay there, grateful as I noted that that my foot and ankle were fine. I imagined I could hear the sheep laughing quietly to themselves. I was humbled.

Living as I do on a farm, I had been flat in the mud before, so I got up and scraped off the mud and went into the house to shower. I couldn't help but imagine what might have happened if I was out in some field in the middle of the night, and I had received a similar mud immersion. No warm shower. No clean clothes. Just move closer to the fire to dry off, and deal with the aroma of dried mud and muck for as long as it lasts. Dirty, wet, and tired, Luke's shepherds were suddenly in the presence of radiant angels! For me, "Fear not!" would need to be replaced with "Do not be ashamed!" Humbling.

To be invited in such a state into the presence of a newborn child or *the* newborn child—whether we consider it metaphor or miracle or both—is a precious thing.

IT'S THE SHEEP, SHEEPIEST TIME OF THE YEAR

On Christmas Eve, I get to play a sheep in the church pageant. A few years ago, our congregation began to hold an "Everybody's Christmas Pageant." Anyone who would like to do so picks a role. One might think it would be natural for me to be a shepherd, but no. I am a shepherd for 364 days of the year. On Christmas Eve, I become a sheep.

For most folks, relative to the rest of year, Christmas is the sheepiest time. Except for the possibility of a summer fair,

Christmas is the one time of year that sheep are all around us. It is easy to find cards with sheep on them, carvings of sheep in stores, and even sheep statues on people's lawns. I have sheep ornaments hanging all over my Christmas tree. In church we sing sheepy carols and read one of the best known sheepy biblical passages: "In that region there were shepherds living in the fields, keeping watch over their flock by night" (Luke 2:8).

Several years ago I brought a lamb to church for our Advent workshop, with the invitation for folks to dress up like shepherds and get their pictures taken with a sheep instead of—or more likely in addition to—Santa. We set up a little wooden pen in the church basement. I brought a supply of hay to keep the lamb occupied and to add to the shepherding imagery. Families lined up for pictures. The lamb enjoyed the whole process too, probably because every child who posed with her offered a handful of grain to keep her calm. She became one of the most people-friendly ewes in the flock.

On Christmas Eve, I lay aside my shepherd ponderings to become a sheep. I find myself looking at life, briefly, from the other side of the rod and staff. As a sheep, I know I have a place in the story. It's a nice, low-key place. As a sheep, I don't have any lines. I can relax and let the shepherds tell me what to do. As a sheep, I have company. Other sheep flock around me. As a sheep, I find myself reflecting on the other very sheepy biblical text, probably the best known one. As a sheep,

I am reminded that God is my shepherd, and I shall not want. I will have green pastures, still waters, and a restored soul.

I do love being a shepherd. I love the rhythm of the life I have made for myself. I love the groundedness I feel when I go about my daily chores. I love the partnership I feel with the sheep, my dogs, and the land. I love being a shepherd in my congregation as well. Praying at the bedside of someone recovering from surgery, blessing a newborn baby with the water of baptism, sitting with someone at the end of life, meeting with my Bible study group weekly, leading worship on Sunday mornings. All of my shepherding church work fills me with a sense of sacred partnership.

On Christmas Eve, though, I love being a sheep.

SILENT NIGHT, SINGING MORN

It's said that the hymn "Silent Night" was written in haste on a Christmas Eve when the organist had discovered that the organ wasn't working for the midnight service. Apparently mice had eaten through the bellows, and no air could get through the pipes. The organist took a poem he knew, quickly composed a melody that could be accompanied by guitar, and the popular hymn was born.

I live on a farm. I've seen how mice can eat through things they have no business gnawing on. One winter they destroyed the wiring in my pickup truck. Knowing what I do about mice, and knowing also how much creativity can be unleashed by the pressure of a last-minute need at a Christmas Eve worship service, I find the story totally believable, even if it is most likely a legend.

This legend came to mind for me when I arrived at church very early one Sunday morning, two days before Christmas Eve, and discovered a stranger standing at the door waiting for someone to let him in. He introduced himself and told me he was there to repair the organ.

The Sunday before Christmas is a big one in my congregation, as it is in many churches. We save up our singing energy for our favorite carols, and then when it seems the energy cannot be contained any longer, we burst out in full Christmas carol mode. That year, we had been referencing the carol "It Came Upon a Midnight Clear" throughout Advent, but we had held back from singing the entire carol. As we approached the final Advent service, the whole congregation was eager to let loose with a full-throated harmonization on all the verses of the carol, accompanied energetically by our talented organist.

Please, sir, repair our organ.

"Where are the bellows?" the repairman asked as I unlocked the doors. "I think I know what the problem is." I had no idea where to send him. Then Tim arrived, one of the volunteer crew that shows up early on Sunday mornings to open all the locked doors. He knew where to find the bellows.

While Tim took the repairman upstairs to examine the inner workings of the organ, I went on with my own Sunday morning preparations. Before long, I received word that indeed the bellows were the problem. The issue wasn't mice. It was age.

Our organ was an old instrument in need of major repairs. During my first Christmas Eve service with the congregation, a note on the organ got stuck and played all the way through one of the hymns, then carried on its own solo performance after every other sound had stopped. Finally, after many years, organ repair was one of the top items on the church's "to do" list, and we had the funds. The repair wasn't scheduled until the following spring, but then an old seam on the bellows ripped on this Sunday two days before Christmas Eve.

Tim called his wife Betty, who brought a sewing machine. They set up a repair station in the fellowship hall to get things sewn together in time for worship. There was a frantic calm when I checked on the progress. Betty was bent over a heavy canvas tube, inspecting the seam she had just sewn, while the repairman suggested adding another row of stitches "just in case." An hour later, as worship began, Betty and Tim and the repairman had accomplished their task. The notes of the organ prelude welcomed the congregation in. With full voices, we sang all the verses of "It Came Upon a Midnight Clear," to wonderful organ accompaniment.

At the end of the service, Bob, one of our parishioners came forward with his guitar. His daughter was with him. He began strumming quietly. It was not "Silent Night" Bob was playing, though. It was his own original song, written a few years prior for a Christmas pageant. He and his daughter sang through the first verse, to let the congregation get the feel for it. Their soft voices were beautiful:

A long time ago, the story says
A baby was born
To a poor girl and a carpenter
And that was Christmas morn.

Our music director Heidi invited all those who had sung this song in the Christmas pageant over the years to come forward and stand with Bob, singing together. My eyes got misty as they sang:

No inn was found to hold the three
So they laid him in a stall
But, oh, the love that was born that day
The world can't hold it all.

The congregation joined:

Came shepherds, yes, and wise men too
And on their knees they fell
And wherever people live in peace,
They worship him as well.
Did angels sing to worship him?

In song his birth proclaim?
If we ever truly touch his grace
An answer will be plain.

Maybe this song will have its own a legend one day. Maybe people will say he wrote it on the spot, when the organ bellows failed. Maybe the story will be that the congregation rose spontaneously, knowing it in their hearts before it came to their lips. Maybe people will say the miracle was that the organ bellows were repaired at the last minute, so the organ joined us all on the last verse of the song. Any of those tales would certainly capture the wonder of that moment, as we all sang together:

Our wish for you this Christmas Day
Is that you will find the star
That shone up over Bethlehem
Shining in your heart!"[1]

---

1. Written by Bob Perkins. Reprinted with permission. All rights reserved.

Church Time

EPIPHANY

❖

❖

Farm Time

JANUARY

AFTER CHRISTMAS

Christmas is such a big event. It can be hard to let it go. I leave my tree up as long as I can without violating some sort of fire code. Nevertheless, sooner or later we take down our Christmas trees, put away the crèches, and move out of the Christmas season into a different time. The season of Epiphany begins on January 6th each year, when the magi followed a star to find baby Jesus—the predicted new king. It ends on Ash Wednesday, when the church shifts to the season of Lent.

In January when I get up early to do my farm chores, I notice that it is just a tiny bit lighter out than I expect. A sliver of moon in the eastern sky greets me, and below her the bright planet of Venus shines. Below them both, the horizon begins to lighten.

"Epiphany" has Greek roots and means to show, or make known, or reveal. We all have experienced epiphanies—those moments of insight when we see something in a new way. The Greek root can also be translated "torch," and it evokes for me an image of a shepherd out in a field on a dark winter morning, swinging a lantern over a stone wall to check on the sheep. "Arise, little sheep, and shine. Your light has come."

My animals may or may not know when Epiphany comes, but they do notice the return of the light. The rooster crows earlier. The sheep start longing for their breakfast, and I imagine they are looking up toward my bedroom window to see if I have started to move yet. The dogs get restless to go out and begin their day. Light returning earlier each morning makes a difference out here.

Sometimes it takes a while for us human beings to notice. We wait for an epiphany of our own, for the assurance that no matter how long the night might seem, the light will return. In the biblical story, the baby and his family, who were cuddled up warm and safe in a stable on Christmas Day, soon find themselves fleeing for their lives. The magi's visit to honor the baby has aggravated the current brutal ruler. The epiphany of love disrupts the powerful of the world, putting everyone at risk.

Although New Year's Day comes before Epiphany, it shares the same kind of energy. New Year's Day on Whidbey Island includes the annual Polar Bear Plunge at Double Bluff Beach. The Whidbey Island plunge was five years old when I discovered it, and I quickly adopted it as my island New Year's tradition.

The first year my sister and I participated, the air temperature was 21 degrees, which made the 45-degree water temperature seem balmy. Nevertheless, it took genuine fortitude to jump in. The following year, the air temperature was twenty degrees warmer, so more people showed up and the atmosphere was more social. I overheard one woman say that she did this dive every year. "It's my annual baptism. I feel like I go into the water and wash the old year off. Then I come back out feeling new."

You can't say "baptism" around a preacher without getting her thinking. Baptism is one of two sacraments commonly recognized in Protestant traditions; the other sacrament is communion. Sacraments are often defined as "a visible sign of an invisible reality." I think of sacraments as mystical moments designed to make the intangible tangible, to help human beings participate with the Holy. Standing on the beach in the cold, shivering, waiting to get even colder, I thought about baptisms and my own motivations for participating in this plunge. Jumping in ice-cold water on an ice-cold day to begin the year was, for me, a way of waking up, of connecting with myself, of marking a moment.

In some ways, my own baptism, at age sixteen, was the same thing. Like at the Polar Bear Plunge, I was dunked all the way under the water. The water of my baptism wasn't cold, though; it was nicely heated and indoors in a warm little church in California. Nevertheless, it marked a moment of waking up and of connecting. The connection at that moment of baptism was with more than myself. There was a preacher, lowering me down in the water and lifting me up. There was a community, watching, praying, and singing from the pews. And there was a tradition, thousands of years old, stretching backwards and forwards, tying me into something bigger than myself.

These days when I baptize folks, it is almost always in a warm church. It is usually an infant who is being baptized, with a light sprinkling of water on the forehead. Still, as a community, we are recognizing a moment of sacred connection. We are celebrating something beyond ourselves, a blessing, a gift, a wonder.

Standing with my sister and two hundred other people on New Year's Day, getting ready to take the plunge, it felt like I was preparing for a kind of self-cleansing. What I really like about the Whidbey Island plunge, though, is the community. Community is what made the beach gathering feel like church.

A horn blew to mark the beginning, just like three chimes of an organ. All of us waded in together. Some people jumped right in and swam out far before turning around and heading back. Others went in so slowly that the rest of us were in and out before they were even up to their ankles. One little kid got his feet wet, then ran out, too cold to continue. I watched my sister go first, then I walked out about fifty feet. Turning around to face the shore, I let myself fall backward into the water. It was just like I fell in my church baptism, but this time without the preacher's arms to lower me and raise me again. I plunged myself under, and then I stood up and hurried out, my feet aching with cold before I got back to the shore. Once I was out, I stood with my sister to encourage the others still taking the plunge.

When it was over, we were all laughing and cheering and congratulating each other. Coffee, hot chocolate, and t-shirts were shared to commemorate the day. Some folks on the beach who had come to watch wondered out loud if they might give it a try next year. Then we all headed home, the community dispersing for another year. I would see those folks around the island all year long, and I would remember this gathering. They were a community for me, like my other community in Seattle, that would remind me to wake up to the sacred all around me, in every moment. I was moving into the season of Epiphany, the time of knowing.

As I watched the crowd head for their cars, I wanted to offer a benediction, like I do at the end of worship services in Seattle: "May you take from this place a sense of love, and grace, and strength, and comfort, that will carry you, until we gather again."

BE THE SHEPHERD YOU WANT TO SEE IN THE WORLD

On the farm this week, the ice is thawing and the rains are coming down. The sheep continue their daily march from the barn to the field and back to the barn. The watching coyote has appeared on the upper field in the middle of the day to remind me that his whole pack is still out there, checking on my faithfulness to the flock. The daily chores continue, no matter what else might be happening around me. The farm work keeps me steady as I prepare for what might come. The nature of the work is not unlike the work I continue to do in the wider world and within my own soul. If you call my phone and I don't answer, you will hear, complete with the sounds of bleating sheep, "I'm out in the barn doing chores or something." That about sums it up.

In dark months like January, as in desolate times in the world, I cherish my daily chores. The simple needs of the flock remind me of what matters most, and of who I want to be. When I was in motorcycle school fifteen years ago, I was taught that, in order to avoid a crash, one needs to look not at what one wants to escape, but in the direction one wants to go. "Your bike will go where you are looking," our instructor explained. "If there is something in the road you want to miss, or if there is something happening up ahead that you want to get around, don't put your focus there. Instead, look to where you want the bike to go."

Whenever I can, I ride a motorcycle from my farm to my church in Seattle. By Washington State Ferry policy, motorcycles go to the front of the ferry line and always get on the boat that is there at the dock. Even if there is no more room for cars, a motorcycle can always squeeze in. This policy has saved me countless hours as I have headed down the hill from my house, past a long line of cars, and onto the boat. When I'm heading home, the motorcycle gets me into the carpool lane and onto the next boat over to the island, no matter how long the wait is for folks in their cars.

Riding a motorcycle can be tricky, and those wise words from years ago—to look where I want to go rather than at what I want to avoid—have saved me from disaster more than once. Still, in high-stress situations on the bike, it is easy to forget. I find myself focusing precisely where I don't want to go. "Watch out," I say to myself as I give my attention over to that thing in front of me that I don't want to happen. The more I give myself to it, the more I find myself heading right where I don't want to be. Then, somehow, I hear the voice of my instructor whispering to me, "Look up. Look beyond. See where you want to go."

In my wider work I have learned, "Be the change you want to see in the world. These words are usually attributed to Mahatma Gandhi, but as it turns out, he never actually said them. What he did say was, "We but mirror the world. All the tendencies present in the outer world are to be found in the world of our body. If we could change ourselves, the tendencies in the world would also change. . . . We need not wait to see what others do."[2]

---

2. *The Collected Works of Mahatma Gandhi, Volumes I–XII* (1884–1914), edited by Indian Ministry of Information and Broadcasting (Delhi, India: Publications Division, 1958–1964).

On the farm and beyond, I am called to keep doing my own inner work of transformation. I claim my own story, rather than allowing someone else to shape the narrative of my life. I continue to live in the light and the hope of my faith.

FEED MY SHEEP

The setting is the Sea of Galilee. It is a resurrection appearance of Jesus, and a conversation with the disciple Peter. According to the story, just days earlier, Peter had denied three times that he knew Jesus. Now, out by the sea, Jesus and Peter are talking again. Peter might have preferred to avoid this thing between them, but Jesus brings it up. "Peter, do you love me?" Jesus asks three times. In my mind the ask is tender and quiet. "I am willing to repair this," Jesus seems to be saying. Each time, when Peter says, "You know that I love you," Jesus responds, "Feed my sheep."

It is a metaphor, of course. There are no literal sheep in this story and Peter was a fisherman, not a shepherd. Nevertheless, the images of sheep and shepherd run deep enough through scripture, so much that "shepherd" became the metaphor for pastors.

I was thinking of all of this one winter Friday while loading hay. As I lifted bale after bale onto my trailer, the phrase

"Feed my sheep" kept running through my mind. What a lot of work that one simple shepherding requirement has turned out to be. I am always on the lookout for hay.

Several years ago, a reality TV show called "Frontier House" challenged families to live as though they were 1880s homesteaders. Would any of them survive a year? After months of hard work, with the families facing and overcoming—or being overcome by—many hardships, and with winter closing in, the show's judges announced their decision. None of the families had succeeded. None of them would have lasted the winter, because none of them had managed to gather enough food for their livestock. Despite their desperate efforts to grow and store lots of grass, "You just don't have enough hay," was the verdict. I am always on the lookout for hay.

When my neighbor called to ask if I was interested in some hay she had for sale, I had immediately said yes. She needed to move four-and-a-half tons of the stuff as soon as possible to make room for a new shipment. That translates to 118 bales of hay lifted out of one barn, stacked on a trailer, driven less than a mile, lifted off the trailer, and stacked in another barn. Mine.

For the first load I had some help. My sister and my friend Meighan had come to the island for the New Year's Day Polar Bear Dive, and I convinced them that moving hay would be a great way to get warm again after our plunge into the cold waters of Puget Sound. We moved about a half-ton that day. For the second load, my island friend Lori helped move another half-ton before picking up her kids.

I loaded and unloaded the next two tons by myself. With hay covering me from head to toe and working its way down into my boots, I began thinking again about that "Feed my sheep" phrase. I guess theological reflection is what we preacher types do when we're so physically exhausted; we are not sure how we will continue.

Feeding sheep seems like such a simple and straightforward task. The reality of what it takes to accomplish it is so much more. "Feed my sheep" is not a one-time thing. Sheep have to eat every day. I have moved tons of hay in the past, and I will move tons more. Isn't that true in our spiritual work as well? As much as we might imagine that a one-time spiritual insight might fill us up and keep us full, we will all get hungry again.

That moment each morning when I carry the hay from my barn to the feeder for the eagerly waiting sheep might be the most satisfying part of "Feed my sheep" work, but it is only one very small part of the job. . There are the folks who worked to grow this hay, watching the skies all summer to know when to plant and when to harvest and when to bale. If the weather turns at the wrong time, or they guess wrong about the baling, the whole crop might be lost. There are the folks who bought the hay from the growers and brought it to market, trying to offer a fair price and to ask a fair price in return. They too will have muscles that ache and hay in their hair and in their boots and anxious days before their work is done. There is me with my friends, loading it all up, carrying it to the barn, and stacking it there.

One of my nephews once said to me, when he was very young, "I like your church job, Aunt Catherine. You only have to work for one hour on Sunday." Of course he had not seen all it takes to get to that one hour on Sunday morning. In the sheep feeding work of ministry, he had only seen the hay carried to the field and tossed into the feeder for the hungry flock. He had not accounted for the growing, the baling, and the stacking of the hay.

After all my hay moving on Friday, I got up early on Saturday morning to travel to a church meeting in Seattle. We spent the first half of a beautiful day huddled indoors looking at spreadsheets and working through agendas to help the congregation be ready to do its justice work in the world. I felt like I did in my neighbor's barn, doing some heavy lifting with an amazing group of folks so that, when the time came, we could carry a little more food from our own church-barn out to a waiting flock.

I am always on the lookout for hay.

CHOP WOOD, CARRY WATER, DO JUSTICE

Before enlightenment, chop wood, carry water.
After enlightenment, chop wood, carry water.
— Zen proverb

Farm chores have to be done every day.
—Farm proverb

It is hard to know whether rain or cold makes life harder for a shepherd. When the temperature drops into the 20s, every outdoor hose, water trough, bucket, and dish freezes solid. I do not want to get up and do my chores. On the farm, though, every day, the animals need to be fed. Even more importantly, every day, they need their water.

When the weather is frigid, the relentless task of carrying water, every day, becomes grueling. It is dark when the alarm rings, and my bed is so warm. I know that I will have to put on several layers of jackets and coats, and a hat and gloves, just to open the door. Even then, the cold will seep through, and my hands and face will be numb before my work is finished. Freezing weather doubles the time it takes me to finish my morning chores. Still, there is something affirming about a shepherd's work in the winter. Caring for my flocks in warm weather is one thing. Remaining faithful to the tasks even in the cold takes me to a new level of my "daily chores" spiritual practice.

Farm chores have to be done every day.

Hay is tossed to the sheep every day. The chicken feeder is filled and the nests are checked for eggs every day. The horses get their alfalfa every day. The dogs are exercised and fed every day. Some of those days are gorgeous, when the sun is coming up and the air is fresh and the sky is a stunning pale pink and blue.

In the winter here in the Pacific Northwest, I often wake up to the sound of rain. When I lived in the city, a rainy day meant turning up the heat and enjoying an extra cup of coffee before running from the house to the car to go to work. On the farm a rainy day simply means wet chores. Falling water finds its way through my collar and down my neck. Puddled water finds that one little hole in my overworked rubber boots. I slosh as I carry another load of hay out to the sheep. There is mud everywhere.

Of course, there is a deep gift in any work that must be done every day. Even in rain, even in snow, even when the temperature drops into the teens, my chores provide a rhythm and a structure to things. They push me outside into beauty I would never notice if I had waited until the rain stopped or the ice melted or the temperature warmed.

My spiritual life is not so clearly structured. When there are no animals around to remind me of the everyday nature of my spiritual thirst, I can easily let rain or sleet or darkness stay me from the swift completion of my appointed practices. When my schedule is rushed or my mood is gloomy or something "more interesting" catches my attention, I can decide that tomorrow, or even next week, will be soon enough to feed my soul.

The prayer of Jesus that I learned to say when I was very young reminds me to ask for daily bread. The animal in me knows that daily bread is what any hungry soul as well as any hungry body needs. I am at my best when I remember it. I am pushed into truth and beauty I would never see if I had the choice to wait for a more convenient time. No matter what might be happening in the wider world, there are some tasks I am called to do, every day. Every day I am called to do justice, and love kindness, and walk humbly with my God.

Every day I am called to show up, no matter how cold the world has turned, and do my chores.

WAITING FOR THE NORTHERN LIGHTS

Experiencing the northern lights is an event on my bucket list. When I read a friend's social media post that advised, "Look to the sky tonight, Seattleites" with a linked article headlined, "Northern Lights Could Appear Above Washington Tonight," I got excited. A strong solar storm, the article said, had raised the possibility of the aurora borealis appearing in our skies.

The only difficulty, of course, could be the clouds of western Washington. The best day to see the lights would be Tuesday but rain was predicted, so Monday night between 10:00 and 10:30 was the night to look up.

That Monday evening, after I put the sheep in the barn, I walked around the pasture with my dog Buddy and found a nice spot from which to watch. I rechecked my compass to be certain I was looking north. Then I waited. And I watched.

I do not know much about the northern lights. Do they appear suddenly, or does the sky gradually begin to glow and then flare with blue and green and purple? Do they flash briefly like a shooting star, so that I have to be looking right where they are to catch them, or do they last a while, so that, if I go inside for a cup of hot chocolate, I won't have missed them? How clear does the sky have to be?

That night there was a half-moon in the sky, a dim glow through the clouds. When I looked north, there were no stars; I could not tell if it was the darkness of clouds or clear black sky.

I stood and stared. I walked further down the pasture to get a different view. I walked back up to try to stay warm. Nothing. I went in the house and made some hot chocolate, then walked out again. My dog Buddy stood in the darkness with me, apparently curious that we were out there with no sheep and no work to do. I looked north.

Then the clouds cleared and the moon came out. Its pale light shone off the fir and cedar and across the pasture. Everything was black and white and gray and lovely. The wind blew some more, the clouds came back and covered the moon again, and I went inside for the night.

The next day I checked social media to see if anyone had more luck than I and had actually seen the northern lights. No. I rechecked the original post and noticed that the article was a week old. The call to look north had been for the previous Monday night.

Still, that quiet night on the farm, standing in the field with my dog, was a gift. While I will keep hoping to see those northern lights at least once in my lifetime, I also hope I can remember to give myself enough time—any time—to notice the quiet beauty that is all around me, rather than waiting only for the one spectacular sky show I might or might not see.

SNOW DAYS

The snow began late Saturday morning, and for me marked the beginning of a week of frustrated plans. My motorcycle had to stay in Seattle where I had abandoned it that morning after trusting the weather prediction that snow would not start until the afternoon. I have a basic policy that if I have to brush falling snow away just to get on the motorcycle, it's too snowy to ride. A friend gave me a ride to the ferry in his warm car, and I walked the two miles home from the dock after the boat carried me across Puget Sound.

Sunday, Monday, and Tuesday my plans changed by the hour as snow appeared, disappeared, and appeared again. By Wednesday, though, there was a foot of snow at my place, the church building was closed along with Seattle schools, and it was an official "snow day."

A pastor's life consists of a fascinating mixture of extrovert and introvert energy. I make time by myself to study the Bible, then lead a bunch of folks in Bible study. I research, read, and write a sermon, and then spend a couple of hours with a lot of people, talking, singing, and sharing. I sit quietly with someone who is sick or hurting, then go to a fellowship dinner where we are all joking and laughing. The schedule is always full, and I feel busy. In the midst of so much to do, it is difficult to find time for relaxed reflection.

A snow day changes all that. For me, a snow day becomes a slow day and offers an incredible gift of time. On Wednesday I enjoyed my morning chores. The sheep came out of the barn with no hesitation and plowed through deep drifts to get to their hay. The dogs also seem energized by the snow. Mac ran around like he always does. He buried his head in the snow and then burst through it, with an expression on his face that I took for a grin. The older dogs, Lizzie and Buddy, seemed more puppy-like than they had in a while. Only the chickens were slightly subdued by the wet, cold whiteness that had invaded their yard.

That day I had time to sit with my coffee and look out my window and soak in the beauty of the farm. The snow quieted my surroundings and invited me to relax more deeply into the moment. I read and wrote. I went sledding with my friend Lori and her girls, who laughed to see a woman older than sixty speeding downhill on a little plastic sled. After that, I still had time for phone calls and emails and social media, and still more reading. Surrounded by sheep and dogs and time, the snow day was like a sabbatical booster shot.

I know such days are not so relaxing for everyone. Snow and ice, disruption, power outages, and isolation can bring significant difficulties. I was glad to get back to my Seattle flock and extrovert activities when the snow melted. Nevertheless, those few days were filled with the fuel of quiet reflection, for which I was grateful.

FROM SHEEP TO MONKEYS

One midwinter night, tucked in my bed, as sleep was descending, I thought of my sheep. It was raining hard outside and I realized that when I had arrived home, after dark, I hadn't seen the sheep in their usual shelter under the trees. I had been leaving them out the last few days, with my guardian dog Giaco in charge of their well-being. If they weren't under their trees, where were they, then? Were they OK?

The border collies were curled asleep in their beds. I was snuggled under warm blankets. Sleep was so close I could touch it.

But where were the sheep?

I began arguing with myself. "They're fine. Just go to sleep." "No, something might be wrong. Something you could do something about. Go check." "But it's wet out there. And it's so warm and dry in here." "Look, you're not going to sleep anyway. Just get up and check, and then you will sleep well."

Soon I was up and out, coat over pajamas, bare feet slipped into boots, flashlight in hand, looking for sheep. I walked the whole field before I found them, up by the gate right where I had come into the field. Somehow they had managed to elude me as I searched, bringing me full circle before I spotted them. I thought I heard them chuckling as I headed back to the house.

This happened in late January as followers of the lunar calendar were celebrating the unfolding of a new year, from the Year of the Sheep into the Year of the Monkey. In the Chinese zodiac, the cycle of twelve years is represented by twelve animals. The sheep is number eight. The Year of the Sheep is reputed to be one of peace and harmony, marked by creativity and elegance. People born in the Year of the Sheep are said to be calm, kind, forgiving, and loyal.

The Year of the Monkey, on the other hand, is characterized by exuberance and unpredictability. It is a time for taking risks and launching adventures. People born in the Year of the Monkey are said to be fun-loving, clever, and inventive.

Compared to sheep, monkeys might seem to be much more interesting creatures. That is true about many of the animals in the Chinese zodiac. Who wouldn't rather be a horse or a tiger or a dragon, than a sheep? Yet I had enjoyed the Year of the Sheep, and my time with sheep has taught me much. Not unlike most of my life, there is a depth and complexity to be found in these creatures. Sheep have taught me the discipline of suspending judgment and opening my mind and my heart to the possibility of something new. When I stopped assuming sheep were dumb, for example, I was able to see the genuine intelligence of their behavior. When I stopped viewing sheep as followers, I saw their leaders emerge. It was easy to imagine I knew all about sheep when everything I knew was theory, but in the day-to-day contact with and care for sheep, something else has emerged. I am humbled by all the ways sheep have of being in the world. I am reminded again of the complexity of all of life.

Here on the farm, it is always the Year of the Sheep, even when, like that rainy night, their hide-and-seek antics seem more monkey-like. May I always be susceptible to that midnight wakening that drives me out into the cold and rain to check on these animals in my care. May I always be open to learning something new.

Church Time

LENT

Farm Time

FEBRUARY – MARCH

∞

GENTLE LENT

∞

"Lent is not about giving up chocolate."

As Marcus Borg spoke these words to the church study group one Sunday morning, many heads swiveled to look at me where I was sitting in the back row. For that whole weekend this profound theologian, professor, and author had been speaking at our church. Because he spoke in such a clear, gentle, and wise way, Marcus always packed 'em in.

Because it was Marcus saying these words, and because I have made something of a point of giving up chocolate every Lent for the last fifteen years, his statement caused heads to turn. I think some of our folks were hoping for a fight.

Admittedly, I wanted to jump up and give my own little speech. I forgo chocolate for Lent as a Lenten practice of mindfulness. I use the season to pay closer attention to what I am doing in the world. The practice is not a sacrifice (well, not much of one), but rather a putting down of something for a season. I take a break from chocolate to make room to notice all the fullness in my life. That Sunday, instead of defending
st smiled and nodded.

: a season of simplicity, beginning with Ash
and ending with Easter. Though the number of

days is specific (forty days plus Sundays), the actual dates of Lent vary. It all depends on Easter, which in the Western church falls on the first Sunday after the first full moon after the vernal equinox. I love that complex formula for Easter, tying our church calendar to the calendar of earth, moon, and solar system. Like Ash Wednesday itself, it reminds us that we are made from the same dust of creation.

Reminders of our mortality are not popular. On the farm, however, life and death are present all the time. Early in my time as a shepherd I came across a cartoon. Several sheep are standing in a circle. One sheep turns to another one to explain, "We're drawing straws to see which one of us will die today for no apparent reason." As a new shepherd I didn't get it; now that I have a few decades of shepherding under my belt, I understand. Life and death are always linked; the proximity of death during Lent—specifically Christ's death—invites us to pay closer attention to life.

"Paying closer attention," as overwhelming as that might sound, can focus on something as simple as chocolate. When I am not awash in chocolate, I notice the sweetness of peaches and pears. I even taste the subtle sweetness of carrots. When I have given up a sugar-filled dessert, an apple becomes a treat. As winter fades, the whole of creation seems to shout, "Pay attention!" Daffodils come up, if you take time to notice. Morning light comes perceptibly earlier, if you're up early enough to see it. On my farm, ewes that have been with the ram begin to bulge, and on other farms, early lambs are already out frolicking with their friends.

I appreciate what Marcus had to say about Lent. He invited us to deepen our understanding of the words we use about the Christian faith. "Sacrifice" means summoning the courage to focus our lives wholeheartedly on God, or whatever we have found to be Sacred. "Repentance," turning away from misdeeds, includes the discipline of increasing one's understanding and growing a bigger heart (spiritually speaking). Lent provides a season for the gentle work of "wholehearted compassion" and the hard work of "heart growth," if we pay attention.

One year, two weeks before Ash Wednesday, I entered the church kitchen and was confronted by an almost two-foot high chocolate Santa perched on the counter. I have a poet friend who likes to remind me that "the universal is always experienced most clearly in the particular." In that spirit, I took the chocolate Santa from the kitchen into the conference room where a meeting was scheduled to start. Eight people looked in wonder as I placed the Santa in the center of the table. "Is that solid chocolate?" someone asked.

"No, it's hollow," someone else answered, as if solid or hollow would make any difference in how much chocolate any of us were about to eat.

I reverently broke the Santa in half, and we passed the chocolate around like it was communion, each of us breaking off a piece of our own. We did not eat the whole Santa that night, but within two days all that was left of Santa was a solid chocolate oval base about an inch-and-a-half thick.

I find it interesting that a chocolate Santa should appear in a church kitchen in the middle of February. Clearly, he was left over from Christmas. Someone was cleaning out, giving up, paying attention, and letting go of the past season. He was a perfect symbol for Lent. By Ash Wednesday, the last of chocolate Santa was gone, and I stopped eating chocolate once again to make room for the more subtle sweetnesses of life. This is a gentle practice, like the gentle and hard work that comes to any farmer in spring. My heart feels bigger already. So bring on Lent, with all its sacrifice and repentance. Bring on spring, with all its gentle and hard work. Bring on mindfulness, with the possibilities for new life.

YOU HAVE TO DEAL WITH POOP

Late winter is the season when I clean my barn. It is a little like spring cleaning, but I do it a bit before spring to prepare for lambing. When I was in Scotland, I learned from a farmer there that the term "barn" was used to denote storage of hay and farm equipment, while the place where the animals stay is called a "byre." My barn and byre are the same building, with the animals staying in one section, the hay in another, and in the back, all kinds of stuff, even stuff from the farmer who lived here before me. The barn's spring cleaning is actually a cleaning of the byre, where the sheep stay at night. Every year I invite friends to help me, which takes some courage: the courage of friends to walk into such an enormous task, and the courage of the barn owner to let them see the mess and accept their help.

Overall, we have a pretty good time. I rent a little bobcat-style loader for the day, and each of us gets to take our turn pushing and pulling levers to make the machine go forward and backward and turn in circles. We work the pedals to make the bucket go up and down and tilt at various angles. Every year it takes time for us to relearn such four-limb coordination, moving both hands and both feet at once in counterintuitive ways.

Being able to talk about sheep poop without noticing the reactions of people around you (for example, whether or not they stop eating their tasty chocolate pudding) is one of the side effects of being a shepherd. Once a child who was visiting the farm stepped in some poop and then looked up at me, not sure whether to be appalled or to laugh. I said, "If you're going to visit a farm, you have to deal with poop." With that reassurance, she chose laughter.

Cleaning the barn can be a ten-hour job, even with the help of a diesel-burning power scooper and four friends. Poop gets pretty high and deep in a year. We use pickaxes, shovels, and pitchforks to supplement the mighty machine, and the deeper we go, the yuckier everything is. By the end of the day all of us are exhausted, and very smelly, but we do not stop until the barn is clean.

The season of Lent can be a kind of spiritual barn cleaning. Stuff piles up in every life. It takes courage to face it and to clean it out. It takes even more determination to ask for help in the process. But the results of such courage and determination are more satisfying than any clean barn at the end of the day.

MID-MARCH MUDDY

I have heard it said that March is the month God created so people who don't drink can know what a hangover is like. That is definitely true here in the state of Washington, where people grow so deeply tired of winter's overcast sky that they forget what the sun feels like. In March, the rain can come down so hard that even my dogs don't want to go outside, but it is rain we need and I am grateful for it. I fell in love with this kind of weather on my first trip to the Great Pacific Northwest in the early 1970s. I traveled north from Southern California, where it almost never rains, to a region with damp clean air and a rich smell of rain and earth. It was exhilarating.

Rain complicates things, of course. We Northwesterners are an "alternate indoor activity" people. The first question that is usually raised any time we plan something is, "What will we do if it rains?" On the farm, when it rains hard, the sheep gather under the pasture cedar as if they are having a sheep summit. The hay in their feeders turns to green mush. The chickens stay inside their hen house, barely venturing out. Mud marks the sheep path from field to barn and settles into a swamp at the barn door. It accumulates around the watering tubs and the feed troughs, and makes mud soup by the gate. Mud makes it hard for sheep or humans to navigate nimbly. I step out of boots that are stuck fast. I slip in mud and fall backwards, and soon there is a thin layer of mud covering my back from head to toe. In western Washington in March, we live with mud.

Dressing for morning chores in the muddy season can be a challenge. How clean can I stay and still get my work done? When time is tight, it is so much simpler to dress in my church-work clothes and hope for the best. However, it is always a risk. Once I made the mistake of putting on my last clean white shirt before I tended the chickens. It was my final morning chore before driving into Seattle for the day. The chicken yard, like the whole farm, was very muddy. I had the sense to put my barn coat over that white shirt. All I wanted to do was move one rooster to a different part of the chicken yard. When I caught him, though, he turned and pecked me twice, then flapped his mighty chicken wings and flew free. As I let go, I fell backwards into the feathers and the mud. The sleeve of the barn coat scooped mud into the sleeve of my last clean white shirt. I resisted thoughts of making rooster soup and instead went up to the house to scrub the mud off my bleeding hand. I wore a purple shirt to work that day.

My evening chores are no more pristine than the morning, although if everything goes smoothly, I can go into the house and relax within half an hour. I open the barn door, lacing a few feed areas inside with hay or grain, and then open the pasture gate where the sheep have all gathered, ready for me. They stampede toward the good food in the barn and fight their way in.

One night, once the ewes were in the barn and I turned back to the house, I heard a plaintive "baa" coming from the field.

Sheep are not loners. When one stays behind after the rest have left, especially if they have left in a hurry as my ewes do at night, that means the one is in some sort of trouble. From the bleating of this ewe, I could tell that was the case. She sounded pathetic.

It didn't take long for me to find her. She had squeezed her head through the field fencing to get to the grass on the other side. It was definitely greener over there. After she had eaten her fill, however, she had become stuck. She couldn't pull her head back through the woven wire fencing.

I examined her situation and tried to help. I went to the other side of the fence to push her head back through. Not a chance. She did not want to back up, and it is completely unproductive to push on a sheep's head when her feet are planted on the ground and she is pushing the other way.

I came back to her side of the fence, grabbed a leg, and tried to pull her backwards. No luck. She still had three good legs pushing forward, and she seemed convinced that forward was the only way out. Especially with me behind her, she was not going to back up.

I cannot by myself move a 140-pound sheep whose head is stuck in a fence. Of course, that did not stop me from trying, from several angles, over and over. By the time I was ready to try a different option, I was sweating, covered with mud, and seriously considering letting her spend the night there. If she didn't strangle herself or get eaten, maybe she would learn her lesson.

By then, it was 10:00 at night. I could not call anyone, and I could not leave her, much as I might fantasize about it. I had to cut the fence. With a larger hole, maybe I could turn her head enough to force her out. Maybe she would even pull it out on her own. I slid my wire cutters along the side of her wooly neck until I found the wire that was holding her tight. After a few tries, despite her continued fight, the wire was cut. She was free.

Except—she wasn't free. Even though it was now easy, she refused to take her head out of the hole. Again I pushed on her head. Just like before, she pushed back. Again I went back behind her and grabbed a leg. Just like before, she leaned forward on her other three legs. When I finally pulled her backwards enough that her head was free of the fence, as soon as I let go, she lunged back in. More than once. "I am stuck," she had convinced herself.

So there I was, at 10:30 PM now, covered in more mud, feeling more exhausted, and revising every good thought I had ever had about sheep intelligence and my own shepherding abilities. But when you are the only shepherd on a farm late at night with a trapped sheep, able or not, you have to keep trying. One more time I grabbed her leg, one more time I pulled backwards, one more time she freed her head, and this time I kept holding on until I could reach up and turn her nose so that when she lunged forward she would not go right back to where she had been. It worked.

She took a few steps to the side and then stood there, uncertain, but now clearly aware that she was free. I walked through the gate and she followed, a little sheepishly, trying to act nonchalant about everything. When I opened the barn door, she called a greeting to her sisters who were by now settled for the night. They looked up as if to say, "Where have you been?"

"I'll tell you in the morning," I imagined her answering. "Is there anything left to eat in there?"

∞

SHEARING SHEEP

∞

Lent is the season of sheep shearing on my farm. The daffodils are ready to bloom, and the lambs are almost due. The sheep are finished with their wooly winter coats that have grown long and heavy. To shear sheep during Lent seems right. It's that time of year when many of us are weary of the dark, mired in mud, and carrying our own heavy loads.

My Lenten chocolate fast is becoming part of that load. Girl Scout cookies are being sold in the ferry line and in front of my grocery store. We are not even halfway through Lent. Was Ash Wednesday really only two weeks ago? Sigh.

Forty days is such an odd amount of time. It doesn't line up with the typical seven-day week. It's longer than the longest month. Lenten practices don't have a "start on Sunday, end on Saturday" rhythm, nor are they a "for the month of" kind of practice. (As if to give us a loophole in Lent, Sundays are not included in the "forty days" count. From a church perspective, every Sunday is regarded as a celebration of resurrection, so Sunday is never a fast day. If you've given something up for Lent, you can indulge yourself on Sundays.)

Lent's "forty days" come from the Gospel stories about Jesus spending forty days in the wilderness, after his baptism and before beginning his public ministry. Forty was also the number of days it is said to have rained while Noah and his family and all the animals were floating in the ark. Forty was the number of years the Jewish people wandered in the wilderness after escaping Egypt and the number of days Moses spent on Mt. Sinai receiving the Torah. Forty appears so often in scripture, it is assumed to point to something significant. On the other hand, some scholars suggest that "forty" simply represent but "a lot."

I find myself wondering about getting to a halfway point. How did Noah feel two weeks into the flood when his ears were ringing from all that noise? Or Moses, after two weeks on Mt. Sinai—did his fingers get numb from all the writing? How was Jesus doing, out there in the wilderness, hungry and alone and counting the days? I know when my chocolate fast will end, but more often I cannot tell when a struggle will end or when I'm halfway through a difficult season. How do we trust that our loads will be lightened? How do we know when we'll be able to shed our weariness like a sheep sheds its wool at shearing time?

It is a pleasure to watch a good shearer at work, and my friend Eifion is one of the best. Because sheep shearing is so fascinating, and because extra hands on the farm are always welcome, I try to invite a few friends up every year to "watch." Most of the watchers end up getting put to work one way or the other. There are scraps of unusable belly wool to put in bags, fleeces to roll up, ear tags to prepare for last year's lambs, annual shots to give the freshly sheared sheep, and always plenty of barn work.

Some years it has been moms with kids who have come to the shearing. The kids watch for a while and then run off to find something else to entertain them on the farm. One year a woman training to be a nurse joined the adventure. She was just the person to prepare the flock's injections. As Eifion sheared, she drew exactly the right amount of the fluid into each syringe and had it ready to hand to him once the wool was off. Vaccinating has never gone so smoothly nor been as precise as on that day. With the student nurse's able oversight of the process, not only did every sheep get her exact dose, none of us accidentally vaccinated ourselves.

One year, Eifion came on a Tuesday, which is the day my Bible study group meets. I took advantage of the timing by inviting them over. They arrived in carpools just as Eifion was getting started in the barn. Some came, looked in, and then went up to the warm house for coffee and conversation. Others came in and stayed, watching for over an hour as Eifion guided sheep after sheep from the holding pen to the shearing area. He caught each sheep around the neck, turned and flipped it quickly onto its back, and cradled it up against his legs. Then like a barber giving a youngster a buzz cut, he turned on the shears and dove in.

Eifion is a good, quiet, and funny man. He patiently answered questions over and over. "Won't they get too cold once all their wool is gone?" *"No."* "Do sheep bite?" *"No."* "Does the shearing hurt them?" *"No."* "Do you mind having such a crowd watching?" *"No."* Are you sure they won't get too cold?" *"Yes, I'm sure."*

After the ewes and last year's lambs were all sheared, we went out to the ram pen to get my new ram. My previous ram had died the year before, and this new wooly beast had come to my farm just a few weeks earlier. At four years old he had only been sheared once in his life, and his wool was so thick it made it hard for him to move around. The ram was not used to being handled and was very wary as we approached. Eifion, ever the expert, caught the ram easily and guided him toward the barn. The ewes watched in fascination from the other side of the fence.

The ram's wool was so thick that the shears would barely go through it. Instead of coming off as one nice fleece, it came off in heavy, dirty sections. His hooves were so overgrown that even my friend Rock, the podiatrist among us, was impressed; if he had had his toenail tools with him, he would have sprung into action. When Eifion finally finished, though, the ram looked clean and handsome. When we sent him back into his pen, he steadied himself as he got used to being almost forty pounds lighter. Soon he was walking with a jaunty spring in his step.

The shearing was done, and we turned the flock out into the field for their long-delayed breakfast. The ewes crowded the feeders, their newly sheared rear ends lining up neatly.

They all seemed to be happy with their haircuts and ready for spring. Eifion headed off to the next farm. The rest of us gathered in my house to reflect on what we had just witnessed and its Lenten lessons.

My own observation related to the ram: "If sheep don't give up their wool, eventually the wool will be the death of them." Sheep that have been bred for centuries to produce wool are not like sheep in the wild. Wool sheep must be sheared every year, or the weight of the wool will eventually cripple, then incapacitate, and then kill them. If you skip even one year, the wool you get is heavy and dirty and useless.

KNOWING THE FLOCK

Shearing is a time of revealing. Wool can hide a great deal. Most woolly sheep look big and healthy. Yet as the shearer catches each sheep, the holding, handling, and shearing make their true condition known. It is as if the story of their lives is clearer once they have been embraced. Which sheep are thriving? Which ones need more food? Which ewes are carrying lambs?

One stormy, windy year, my shearer Eifion arrived early, since the first farm on his schedule was without power, and his shears are electric. A few folks from church came over on the ferry to help. Eifion set up his shearing station and his shearing pen, packing the sheep tightly inside. From there he took them, one by one, and flipped them on their backs.

The sheep relaxed in Eifion's firm grip and he passed his shears over them. Up the neck at first, then over the head, then what are called the "long blows," as the shears moved down their backs and along their flanks. Almost always the fleeces came off whole, and beautifully rich. As we gathered, rolled, and stored each fleece, still warm as it had come off the sheep, our hands soaked up the grease, or lanolin, that permeated the wool. The lanolin is part of what makes sheep's coats so nicely warm and waterproof. Although it smells distinctly different from the lanolin cream one might purchase, it is just as soothing.

Of the three ewes I put in with the ram that year, two were pregnant. The third one was not. "Too old," Eifion said. "She's got no teeth." Without teeth, she wouldn't be able to eat the amount of nutrition needed to maintain a pregnancy or to feed hungry lambs if they come. I was a bit embarrassed; I should have caught that before I ever put her in with the ram.

One of last year's lambs was too little. She was the one who was last to the feeder, and she was not growing as I wished she would. Her wool was not of much use, and her small stature was even more pronounced once she was sheared. The next sheep sheared was healthy and robust. Her wool came off beautiful and full.

"There might be a wether in with these ewes," I warned Eifion as he caught and flipped another sheep. If a wether—a neutered ram—is among the ewes, it is helpful for a shearer to be forewarned. "Might be?" he asked. "Don't you know your flock?"

He meant it as a joke, but any suitable shepherd knows how many sheep she has and how they are doing. There are even shepherds who can look out over their flocks and know immediately that one of the hundred is missing. Those shepherds are called "good," and the best shepherd knows not only that one has gone astray, but can tell you if the one that is missing is a ram, a ewe, a wether, or a lamb. That shepherd is the one who will leave the ninety and nine, and head out looking for the one that is lost.

I am a casual shepherd. Yes, I keep an eye on my flock. I keep the rams and the ewes separate except when I want more sheep. I try to count them at the end of the day to be sure everyone is settled and safe. But sometimes, when I come home from my Seattle flock late at night, tired and ready for bed, I glance out at the sheep bedded down under the giant cedar by the fence, and I think to myself, "Yeah, it looks like they're all there." Sometimes I leave a wether in with the ewes and then forget he is in there.

Pulling me out of my reflections, the friend from church who had been measuring the vaccines for the sheep said, "I don't think we are going to have enough for all the sheep."

"Not enough?" I said. "But the box says '25 doses,' and we only have nineteen sheep to dose."

She showed me the bottle. Sure enough, it was low. Suddenly I remembered I had not checked on the dosage. I assumed I knew. "Three cc's per sheep," I had told my friend. But the correct dose was two cc's. The extra vaccine wouldn't hurt the sheep. It was just that now I might run short. Six sheep hadn't been vaccinated yet. Two pregnant ewes were among that lot, and they were the ones that needed this vaccination the most.

As it turned out, we had just enough medicine to vaccinate every sheep.

"Don't you know your flock?" Eifion's question settled into my heart. It was there for these sheared and vaccinated sheep before me. The real question my heart was holding, though, was for my other flock. Do I know them? There are several hundred people in my amazing congregation. Some of them I do know well. Some of them I don't know at all. Sometimes I look out over the congregation on a Sunday morning and think to myself, "Yeah, it looks like they're all there." Sometimes I might notice if someone is not there, especially if they tend to sit in the same place.

There are times, though, that one from this flock will go missing and I don't realize it. One might be having a rough time, but a forced smile conceals it. Sometimes I will think I know what they need, but I'm wrong. Sometimes, in all the distractions of life, I forget to connect.

In the midst of all that, though, I know two things.

The first is that each person in my congregation is unique and remarkable. Even though there are those I don't know personally, I do know that each of them is living a life of challenge, and courage, and pain, and joy. Whenever I sit with folks, and hear their deepest stories, I am moved, and inspired, and connected, and changed. What a gift it is to be a shepherd of two flocks.

The second thing I know is that, whatever kind of shepherd I may be, I am also a part of a flock. There is another Shepherd who truly knows this flock. Even when I am not the shepherd I hope to be, I can trust myself and my flock to that Good Shepherd, who holds me, and my congregation, and indeed the whole world, in Her gentle hands.

FROM SHEEP TO SHEEP

At the state fairs and in the county shows they call the competition "Sheep to Shawl." A team works together to shear a sheep, clean the fleece, spin the wool, and weave it into a shawl, all in a race against the clock. An average competition might set the time limit at two or three hours. Amazing.

I have never seen a Sheep to Shawl competition, but I have seen my sheep sheared, and the fleeces turned into yarn, and the yarn turned into something new. The process takes months.

Sometimes years. Almost a decade ago now, my sister turned some wool from one of my sheep into a lovely vest that she knitted for me. That process took over a year and a half. The end result was beautiful.

One year, John, who is in my Bible study group, asked if I had any wool available. He wanted a skein to give to a friend of his, who he knew loved to knit. I had some lovely brown wool that was unclaimed from the previous year, so I gave it to him. Then I went off on a trip to Wales and Scotland.

When I returned from my time away, John handed me a little bag. "It's a gift from Mieke," he said, naming the friend to whom he had given that skein of wool. I opened it to discover a delightful little lamb, knitted with care, and a note.

"I was a child in Europe during World War II," Mieke wrote, "and I remember how hard those times were. As we grew," she continued, "my mother would unravel our wool clothes and reknit them into something new that would fit our growing bodies. As soon as I held the wool from your sheep, those memories came flooding back. The aroma of lanolin coming off the wool as I wound it into a ball. The feel of the wool as it slipped through my fingers while I was knitting. The natural soft brown color of this wool. All of that reminded me of my family, all together, and doing what we needed to get by. Thank you for those moments of remembering."

She had used the wool that John had given her to knit three little lambs. One for her to keep. One for John. And one for me.

What a surprise. What a gift.

Sometimes the results of our work are right at hand. They are seen quickly, and we can watch as our gifts are transformed. Other times, though, our gift passes through many hands. From the shepherd who has tended the sheep. From the sheep who are glad to be a bit lighter in the spring. From the shearer who comes from Wales and works while his wife visits the home where she grew up. From a small fiber mill, set up by a woman starting a new life on the island. From a friend who knows a friend who likes to knit. Then back around again to the shepherd. We might wait for years for those gifts to come to fruition. The stories of the hands through which our gift passes can be profound. Some of them, if we knew them, would move us to tears. They all remind us again how we are woven together like a shawl.

HOW TO CATCH A WILD RAM

The lone ram lamb is out in the field, watching us warily. When all the other sheep had been gathered in the barn, this fellow had refused to go. He is not quite a year old and has spent the last six months in the ram pen with the other boys, out of contact with people. The ewes move from the barn to the field and back again regularly, following me and the sound of grain rattling in the bucket I carry.

The boys, though, stay outside, in their separate pen adjacent to the barn. Their only contact with me is at a distance, when I throw hay in their feeder. They are all skittish except Junior, the boy we bottle-raised when his mom couldn't feed him. Junior will follow me anywhere. The other boys run when I approach.

On shearing day, Eifion goes to the ram pen after all the ewes are sheared. Folks who have come to help form themselves into a human fence to guide the rams into the barn. Thanks to Junior, the friendly wether, the sheep cooperate, except for this one wild youngster. He has run to the other side of the large pen, and we cannot get within a couple hundred feet of him.

Eifion is smart enough to know it is almost impossible to catch a sheep by itself. A sheep on its own is a sheep in trouble and generally knows it. That lonely sheep will be in maximum flight mode, and to try to catch him now will only make the flight, well, flightier. This ram lamb just earned himself a name: "Trouble." Eifion takes the sheep he has and gets back to work, leaving Trouble alone to calm down.

When all the other boys have been sheared, I put out some grain and hay for them, and they hurry back into their pen through the human fence we have reconstructed. Trouble sees the other sheep with their heads in the feeder and gets curious. He cautiously comes toward his old friends, even while we stand nearby trying to look innocent. He keeps one eye on us, as prey will do around predators.

Early on in my shepherding life, I realized that sheep's eyes are different than mine. Not only are they set on the side of their heads, appropriate for an animal that is always on the lookout for danger, but their pupils are not round. They are a horizontal rectangle. This is why images of sheep looking straight ahead through round eyes look so goofy. Those are human eyes we have given the sheep. But sheep need their horizontal pupils for a certain kind of watchfulness. Horizontal pupils can adapt to sunlight and moonlight. The shape also makes sheep especially good at depth perception as they scan any horizon. Anyone who has ever tried to sneak up on a sheep knows how well sheep eyes function. Trouble is still skittish, and he keeps an eye on us.

A good shearer, by the way, is also a good sheep catcher. Eifion seems magical in his ability to grab sheep as they go by, lifting them effortlessly, and gripping them in an inescapable hold. Trouble is an expert dodger though, and he eludes Eifion again as he runs by him and to the feeder.

Now Trouble is surrounded. The feeder is in front of him, the fence is behind him, and Eifion is coming up beside him. I am standing in the small gap between the feeder and the gate. Only a foolish sheep would think he could get out that way.

Trouble proves himself to be foolish. As Eifion grabs for him, he slips away and runs right toward the gap and me.

In the many years I have been tending sheep I have, by necessity, learned some things about catching them. You have to move fast. You have to hold on to whatever you grab hold of. If you have let a sheep slip away, any next chance you get will be a slimmer one than you had at first. Sheep are quick learners. Therefore, once you have a sheep in hand, do not let go.

As Trouble runs toward me, I move fast. Well, I move fast for a sixty-plus-year-old lady. I jump into his path and grab. I have hold of his leg. We both tumble down into the thick mud, and lie there side by side. I don't let go. Then Eifion comes over and grabs us both, as if we are each about to be sheared. He hands Trouble to my friend John, and he hoists me by the collar until I am standing upright. He jokes that I would have made a good rugby player—high praise from a Welshman.

I am covered in mud, and I am jubilant, as if by catching the ram I have achieved a new level in my shepherding apprenticeship. While Eifion shears Trouble, I go up to the house to shower and change. Trouble comes out of the barn, beautifully clean as freshly shorn sheep are, and I come out of the house, all cleaned up too.

—◆—

Church Time

EASTERTIDE

Farm Time

APRIL

A DANGEROUS TIME OF YEAR

Most years I am well prepared for spring. I live by the rhythm of the year with both my flocks. Pastors count the Sundays of each church season, no matter what the seasons are outside. Shepherds count the months until lambing, planning so the babies are born after the cold goes away and in time for the good grass to be ready when they are weaned.

Church seasons and sheep seasons are mostly painted in broad strokes; exact beginnings and endings can change. I once studied a bud on a bare brown stick. From a distance, the bud looked like just a smudge of color, but through a field glass, the tiny bud was huge and I could see its green life breaking out. The brown husk of the bud looked like a shroud that had broken apart, and it was clear the tiny green leaves could not be contained. Close up, the bud break looked like an explosion.

For Christians in the northern hemisphere, the story of spring is reflected in our story of Easter. As the spring grass turns a pasture green and a brown bump-of-a-bud breaks open on a grape vine, the resurrected life of Jesus bursts from a tomb. Two thousand years later, I can be tempted to believe that the story could be contained in some safe way. But close up, I recognize Easter as an explosion. Easter changed everything for those early followers of Jesus. I am sometimes not sure I want to be changed so dramatically. I have gotten so used to the time of late winter.

The date of Easter Sunday varies, depending on the vernal equinox and the spring full moon. By Easter Sunday, the northern hemisphere has tilted back toward the sun, and each day the light hangs around a little longer. Eastertide follows Easter Sunday on the church calendar and lasts for fifty days until Pentecost Sunday. That was a dangerous time too, according to Luke's account, when the early followers of Jesus were turning the world upside down.

On the farm, the spring season is a dangerous one. New life bursts out all around me. I suspect that, were it not for the church calendar, I would just put my head down, my shoulder to the wheel, my nose to the grindstone, my hand to the plow, and work, work, work without ever noticing the quiet of winter yielding to the blooms of spring.

My sheep help me count the days with intention. I work hard at planning their year, from the quiet summer days when the grass is lush to the early fall when ewes are put in with the ram, and then counting the days until the lambs start to come. I regulate their feed according to that counting, and I hire the shearer according to that counting, and I watch their behavior according to that counting, as lambing approaches.

In my attempts to balance the lives of my two flocks, I try to count the sheep days in conjunction with the church days.

Most critically, I plan my lambing so that no lambs are due on Easter Day. The last thing I want to deal with on Easter morning is a ewe who needs my assistance just as I am supposed to be rushing off to a congregation all dressed up for one of the most significant worship services of the year.

Sometimes, in the midst of our counting, we discover we are in a very different season than we thought we were. That is life. That is its mystery, its delight, and its dismay. Despite my best efforts, there are years when lambing and Easter overlap. One Easter, as I was with my Seattle flock, the ewe who had not yet lambed found her way to the cedar tree that has become a favorite birthing place. There, while I was paying attention to my other flock, she gave birth to her lamb. She did not need my assistance, and I did not even notice when I left early that morning dressed in my Easter best that it was about to happen. It was simply an Easter blessing, and a wonderful surprise, as such blessings almost always are.

THE PUPPY AND THE LABYRINTH

Jake was my first border collie, and I got him just after my young dog Nikki had been hit by a car and killed. Jake was not Nikki, and I missed Nikki tremendously. One evening in my old house in California, sitting on my kitchen floor with the puppy Jake leaning into me, I wept for Nikki. I said through my tears, "I am trying to love you, Jake. If you will hang in there with me, I will hang in there with you. You just have to give me time." In what turned out to be a very short time, I did fall deeply in love with Jake. He remained my good and precious friend for the rest of his very full life. He talked me into moving to a farm and getting my first sheep. He is buried under an oak tree on a farm in Oregon.

On my Washington farm, I had Lizzie and Buddy, but they were getting older too. I needed a young dog to add to the pack. I searched the Pacific Northwest Border Collie Rescue pages regularly for months, until I finally found a dog that seemed right. This pup was from a litter of four on a farm in eastern Washington. I called my new dog Mac after my former colleague Don Mackenzie. When I named my cats Schultz and Fritz after my other colleagues Peter Ilgenfritz and Dave Shull, I made a commitment that my next pet would be named after Don. Mac is a border collie, the "border" part referring to the border hills between Scotland and England, where the breed was developed to work sheep in the hills there. A Scottish name seemed quite appropriate. When Don saw a picture of Mac, he said, "He even looks like me."

I had forgotten how much work puppies are. They chew on everything, they need constant supervision, they have no manners, and they pee and poop all the time. I had also forgotten how hard it is to let go of one image of "good dog" to make room for another. I had forgotten how deep feelings of loss and hope get mixed up with each other. I had forgotten how sharp the pain can be, and how hard it is to find the faith to open up again.

Just a few days into my new life with little Mac, it was clear to me that I had some internal work to do to bring my full heart to this adventure, so I went up to the labyrinth on my farm. Labyrinths can be wonderful tools for the spiritual practice of letting go and opening up. Mine is a small, seven-circuit design that a friend helped me build near the woods above my house. This labyrinth does not take long to walk, and it has been a very helpful place for me to listen to my life.

I went to the labyrinth with the very specific purpose of letting go of my expectations for Mac, so framed by my love of Jake, and opening myself to this new dog. Mac and my two older dogs, Lizzie and Buddy, came with me. When we arrived, Buddy curled up outside the labyrinth, Lizzie went off exploring, and Mac followed me to the entrance. I paused, took a deep breath, and began to walk. "Letting go," I said to myself as I exhaled.

My labyrinth is made of long cedar branches that curve wonderfully to form a circular path. Mac picked up the first branch he saw and began to drag it off. "No," I said, taking it from his mouth and putting it back where it belonged. I continued to walk. Mac, trotting behind me, spotted another branch and sank his teeth into it. "No," I said again. "Leave it." He put his front paws down, and, with his rear end up in the "let's play" pose, he wagged his tail. I reached for the branch and he jumped back away and out of reach. The branch was very long, though, so I caught the end of it, pried it from Mac's mouth, and put it back in place. As Mac reached for it again, I picked him up and kept walking, carrying him away from his newfound toy.

When we reached the other side of the labyrinth, I put him down again. He ran over to where Buddy had fallen asleep and started barking. "Letting go," I repeated to myself as I tried not to listen to the barking. I walked on.

At the center of my labyrinth is a heart shaped rock-bowl, and in it I have placed a lovely brass bell that I found out in the field. I am not sure how this delightful little bell got out there in the first place. It is not a sheep bell. After I found it, the labyrinth seemed the perfect place for it; ringing it has become another part of my labyrinth ritual. As I arrived at the halfway mark of my "labyrinth walk for Mac," I paused meditatively, then picked up the bell, rang it, and set it back down. Mac immediately stopped barking at Buddy and came tearing back into the labyrinth. He grabbed the bell and ran.

Dog trainers will tell you it is a bad idea to chase a puppy. Chasing teaches the puppy to run away from you, and it is almost always futile. Humans are not as fast as puppies, and Mac was especially fast. So in spite of my rising frustration and the temptation to give chase, I turned and ran in the opposite direction, calling, "Come on Mac" in as cheerful a tone as I could muster. It worked. He turned in an instant and, with the bell clinking dully in his mouth, raced toward me. As he dashed past, I caught him and lifted him up, causing him to drop the bell. With Mac wiggling in my arms, I returned to the labyrinth's center. "Letting go," I said to myself again. I stood there holding my squirming puppy until he settled, and waited a bit longer until I did too. Then I started on the path out.

As I walked out, I said to myself, "Opening up." Mac relaxed more, and leaned into me in a way that reminded me of that moment with Jake so many years ago. "Yes Mac," I said, "opening up. To you." I gave him an extra hug and let him slip down out of my arms.

As he ran off to get into some other kind of mischief, and as I finished my seven circuits out, I began to smile. Then I started laughing.

∞

LAMB WATCH

On my farm, Eastertide means lambs. Most Pacific Northwest sheep have their lambs in February or March, when the weather warms just enough for everyone to avoid freezing and the green grass will be available by the time they are weaned.

Lambing time on my farm is tied to a different, more liturgical schedule. My attention is very focused on my Seattle flock as Easter approaches. I have found through the years that unless Easter is unusually late, it is easier to wait until after that date to focus on my sheep. Lambing time, even with a flock as small as mine, is intense, and exhausting, and wondrous. It demands attention.

Several years ago, after I came home from work, certain that I would find lambs in the field, I looked out and saw only full-grown sheep looking back at me. My ewes appeared so ready to give birth, and I had been hurrying back to my farm day after day, eager to be certain that all was well, expecting each time to see lambs. There is nothing that warms a shepherd's heart in spring more than the sight of a ewe calmly watching her babies struggle to their feet.

These ewes, however, still had not given birth. Frustrated, I grabbed my camera and took a picture of them, all lined up and staring at me. On a whim, I posted it on social media with the caption, "No lambs." I thought the waiting would end quickly. In fact, I wondered if I would have a chance to post another "No lambs" picture before the births began. I've been through lambing before, and I should have known: sheep have their own timetable.

The next time I checked on everyone, later that night, there were still no lambs. On social media, people were waiting to hear from me. Several asked me to keep them informed of any lambing progress. I decided to post a status update and a picture every time I checked for lambs.

Again, I thought it would only be a matter of days until the lambs came. Again, I was wrong. As I waited and posted, all kinds of folks began to join me with their support, their empathy, and their humor. "Are you sure they are pregnant?" someone asked. One cynic suggested the ewes were simply waiting until the wettest, darkest, coldest part of the most inconvenient night to lamb. She must have spent time on a sheep farm.

Through the days and even in the middle of the night, I posted updates. "We're all waiting with you," a Facebook friend said. The wait had turned from lonely vigilance to community project. My sister, a midwife in Oregon, noted, "Just like my work."

A week went by. The number of folks on "Lamb Watch" continued to grow. My niece wrote, "Aunt Catherine, your lamb statuses are keeping me quite entertained! Another friend empathized with the sheep as much as the shepherd: "Poor fat sheepies. Have your babies!"

As the days went on and my posts multiplied, folks continued to express everything I feel during lambing time. "I'm confused. Will there ever be lambs?" asked someone. In solidarity, one of my parishioners asked, "Is this the longest you've ever had to wait, or just the longest *I've* ever had to wait?"

Early in the morning, ten days after Lamb Watch started, I finally had a different post: "Lambs. Born earlier this morning. One was there when I checked at 2:30, the other was born as I was watching the first one try to stand. Thanks all."

A parishioner answered with a reverent and appropriate, "Hallelujah!"

Four years after the first Lamb Watch, at the vernal equinox, as the first day of spring was dawning, my first lamb of the year was born. I wasn't expecting her so soon. Nevertheless, there she was, standing by her mother's side. She had that stunned blinking look of a creature who is new to this strange, bright world and is wondering what on earth just happened. Mom was busy welcoming her by cleaning her off and making those incredible, soft chuckling sounds ewes make to their lambs. I never get tired of hearing that gentle first conversation. The little lamb was not much more than an hour old. She was standing, which lambs do pretty quickly after they're born, but she hadn't been cleaned up much yet. Her mom kept working on that as I walked up to her. Immediately after lambing, ewes are surprisingly calm. There is no other time when I can walk right up to my sheep. Usually they run in the opposite direction when I try to get near. But when a ewe has lambed, her focus shifts. She stays right there with her baby, no matter how close I get. I believe she knows I'm there to help. More likely her nonreaction to my presence is a combination of exhaustion and maternal protection. She simple won't leave her lamb.

The lamb doesn't run from me either. Often, the lamb will do just the opposite, taking unsteady steps toward me, as if to ask, "Are you my mother?" That is what this new little girl did. I scooped her up and carried her to the barn, with mom following right behind. Once they were settled in, with fresh hay and water, I went back to the house and broke the news that Lamb Watch had ended before it even began. I posted a picture of mother and baby on Facebook. "Sorry friends, no Lamb Watch." The reactions were quick. Many celebrated this first lamb, but friends also told me that they had a different sense of this journey.

"When are we going to get another Lamb Watch update?" someone posted the next day.

"Lamb Watch ends when the first lamb is born," I answered.

"No," he responded. "Lamb Watch ends when the last lamb is born."

Lamb Watch was only a three-year-old tradition at that point, and already there was the threat of a schism. It reminded me of my congregation in Seattle, and the way we don't know that something is a "thing" until it changes, or doesn't happen, or someone comments on it. We have the same Christmas pageant two years in a row, and then, the third year when we do something different, folks will inevitably comment on how our "tradition" has changed. Every community has its rules, its "things," its traditions. I'm aware of the courage it takes to be new, to join in—not unlike the courage it takes to welcome change. The shepherd doesn't always set the "rules" or know how they might change. But Lamb Watch is now a tradition on my farm.

LOST LAMB

I should know not to expect to get through my morning chores quickly during lambing season. After I had been on the farm for five years, though, I fooled myself into thinking I could do just that. I got up before dawn that spring morning planning to catch the 7:00 ferry in order to catch the last express bus from the Mukilteo ferry dock into Seattle, in order to be at the church thirty minutes early for a 9:00 AM meeting. I was hoping all would go smoothly with my morning chores, including the sheep chores.

I checked the barn, just to see if any lambs had been born during the night. A new lamb would mean some extra work, but I had allowed time for that. I opened the barn door and swept my flashlight over the flock. All the ewes were lying down, still dozing or just waking up. The only lambs I saw were the three that I already knew about. So I relaxed and went over to the other side of the barn to get breakfast out for the sheep.

I scooped three cans full of COB (a grain mixture of corn, oats and barley) into the bucket and carried it out to the field feeders, then came back for a couple of loads of hay. By the time I returned to the sheep area of the barn to let the girls out for the day, I heard one ewe in great distress. "Baa? Baaa? BAAAA!" she was crying. "Where is my baby?" I translated. I turned the overhead light on and looked around the barn again.

There were the three lambs that had been born over the last week, standing with their moms in the lambing jugs. There were the rest of the ewes. Then there was the one ewe in deep distress. No new lamb in sight. My border collie Lizzie slipped in through the open door to assess the situation. She looked around, then looked at me. "No new lambs here," her eyes said. Still, the cries of the troubled ewe were ringing in our ears.

I had counted the ewes as they came in from the field the night before. I had walked the field that night too, in case some careless first-time mother might have left her baby behind. Still, I questioned myself. Could I have left a lamb out?

Opening the barn door, I let all the sheep except the ewes with lambs stampede out. I was thinking that if the ewe in distress had indeed left her lamb out the night before, she might run to the spot and I could follow her and try to figure out what had happened. But she just followed the others out, took a few bites of hay, and then stood in the middle of the field bawling. "No. This is not what I'm hungry for. Baa! Baaa! BAAAA! Where is my baby?" Still no answer. No lamb.

I returned to the barn and looked around, trying to see if I could find some clue there as to what had happened. I saw a place right by the door where the barn siding had pulled away a little bit, leaving an opening where the wall and the floor of the barn met. Could a lamb fall through there? I got down on my knees and shone the flashlight through the hole and down into the patch of blackberries below. Nothing.

I went outside to examine the other side of the hole. Of course it was raining, and the rain was beginning to soak through my clothes. The opening in the barn wall dropped out into the ram pen. It was still dark, but I crouched down and shone the flashlight under the barn. Nothing. Where else could the lamb be? I crawled through the mud and under the barn and looked around, letting my flashlight play over the old pipes, rocks, and a stack of wood windows the previous owner had stored under there. I saw nothing. Lying there quietly for a minute, I listened carefully. I heard nothing.

The sky was getting brighter. I walked around the ram pen, looking in every corner. Nothing. The calls of the ewe in the field were beginning to sound even more desperate. What could I do? I decided to finish my chores and wait for more light. I wasn't going to make the 7:00 o'clock ferry. So I fed the ram and the wether, fed the other sheep in the pen, fed the dogs, fed the cats, fed the chickens, and gathered the eggs. Then I went back down to the barn, hoping that the lamb had somehow magically appeared. Nothing.

As the sky finally got light enough for me to see without a flashlight, I walked to the big field where the ewes were still eating their breakfast and the forlorn mama was still calling for her baby. While she called out, she trotted first one direction, then the other. She was on the edge of pure panic. I walked the whole field again, this time with my dogs Lizzie and Buddy. If there was a lamb anywhere in the field, Lizzie for sure and maybe Buddy too would spot it. There was no trace of a lamb, however, and no scent of one either as far as I could tell from the dogs' behavior. I went back to where the sheep were feeding, and when I opened the gate and headed back to the barn for one more look there, the sad ewe ran back with me.

"Was there really a lamb?" I began to ask myself. "Could the ewe have had some sort of false pregnancy or miscarriage, and now just thought she had a lamb somewhere? Does that happen with sheep? Or if she had delivered a lamb, could it have been carried off by eagles? Coyotes? Something?"

The only place I could think to look again was under the barn. With gloves on and clippers in hand, I cut my way through the blackberry bushes under the hole in the barn siding, imagining maybe I had missed the lamb in there. Nothing. Then back under the barn I went, by now too wet and muddy to care that I was just getting wetter and muddier. Another sweep of the flashlight, since it is dark under my barn even when it is light outside. Nothing.

The other ewes in the barn with their own little lambs were getting restless with the sound of this sad one calling and calling. They were also the last group for me to feed, and they were ready for breakfast. I gave them their COB and their hay, and they settled in to eat. Even the ewe with the missing lamb, maybe exhausted by now, began quietly eating. My heart was breaking for her. "I'm sorry," I thought. "I have done everything I can think of to find your lamb, and I just can't do it. I wish I was a better shepherd. I don't know what else to do."

I was too late for the bus now, so I would be on my motorcycle, in the rain. Before I turned to leave, I stood for one last moment in the silence of the barn, listening to the ewes quietly chewing their hay, feeling the sad ewe's heartbreak and my own.

When I had completely let go of hope, and when the mama ewe was trying to comfort herself by eating, I heard it. A tiny "baa." That sweet and plaintive cry of a newborn lamb, calling for its mom. Or maybe it was my young rooster, who is still learning to crow. Or the geese that have been flying low over my farm the last several days, calling to each other as they go. Or my deep desire to hear something was toying with my imagination. Or maybe it *was* a newborn lamb.

I kept listening. "Call again, please, call again." I prayed. There it was—a bit stronger this time. Definitely a lamb. But where? The sound was still so faint that I could barely sense what direction it was coming from. I walked around the barn, looking and listening. Could the sound really be coming from underneath? After I had already been under there twice, could there still be a lamb down there? Maybe.

I got my dog Lizzie and crawled under the barn one more time. "Sheep?" I asked her. "Where's the sheep?" Responding to her invitation to work, she did what she always does when I talk to her that way: she found the sheep.

It was a little ewe lamb, jet black, blending into the darkness and hiding in the farthest corner, where I had pointed my flashlight twice and never seen her. Earlier, having seen nothing and heard nothing, I had not crawled all the way back to look behind the rocks and the pipes and the other stuff there. Now, there was Lizzie, doing her border collie stare, and the little lamb, looking back and calling louder: "Maa! Maaa! MAAAA!" I got close enough to catch her, and holding her tightly, crawled out from under the barn, through the mud and into the light. "Good dog, Lizzie," I kept saying, realizing what an understatement that was.

Walking with the lamb in my arms back into the barn, I was deeply grateful. But I also knew there was one more hurdle for her. If she had been away from her mom for too long, her desperate mother might now refuse to recognize this lamb as her own. When I went into the barn with this little one, however, who was now calling "Maaaaaa" at the top of her lungs, the ewe ran right over to us and answered "Baaa, baaaa" to her baby. Then she said, "Baaaa, baaaa, baaa" to me too.

I was so relieved I was shaking. I caught my breath and put the little lamb down. Immediately her mom began to nuzzle her, and the lamb began to nurse. It was the scene I love most during lambing, a contented mother with a healthy lamb beside her nursing hungrily.

Lizzie was by my side, looking on. "Good dog, Lizzie," I said again, and then went up to the house, washed off as much of the mud as I could, changed my clothes, got on my motorcycle, and caught the 8:00 o'clock ferry into work. I was only a little late to the 9:00 o'clock meeting.

ONE MORE LOST SHEEP SERMON

Lost sheep are a regular part of shepherding, and shepherds who know Jesus' parable of the Lost Sheep in Luke 13 have regular opportunities to reflect on it.

One spring evening several years back I let the sheep out for the evening to graze the upper pasture for an hour before they would go into the barn for the night. I stood at the gate watching them disappear up the drive, and prepared to follow. I try not to leave them alone when they are in that pasture near the woods, where hungry coyotes have been known to wander.

As the flock rounded the big blackberry patch, I heard behind me the panicked baa of a lamb. I turned and saw the little one, coming up from the farthest corner of the lower pasture, and running as fast as she could to the gate. Perhaps she was sleeping when everyone left, or maybe she had been off playing by herself when suddenly she looked around and discovered she was alone.

By now the rest of the flock was not only out of sight but out of hearing as well. Usually when a lamb calls as plaintively as this one, a mother answers right away. But there was no answering "baa;" no "I'm over here" call. This mom either couldn't hear the cry, or, more likely, felt that this lamb was old enough to find her own way. Maybe mom had just gotten tired of tracking this lamb all over and decided she might need a lesson in "staying found."

There was only the sound of the little one, who had stopped at the gate and was looking and calling desperately while running back and forth, not sure where to go. I hoped I could steer her to the upper pasture. After all, she had been up there before. But she seemed convinced that the rest of the flock must be somewhere in the lower pasture, so she continued to dash all around down there, calling and looking. Then she ran into the barn, hoping she might find someone there. The barn was empty too.

So here was a new twist on the lost sheep story. I knew where the lamb was, so in that sense she was not lost, nor alone. She, however, did not know where the flock was. She did not know where her mom was. I, the shepherd, was of no comfort to her. I just looked like one more threat.

I found myself envying the shepherd in Jesus' parables who, if the Bible pictures are to be believed, found the lost sheep caught in brambles, dangling off a cliff. At least that lost sheep was immobile and could be lifted and carried home. This little lamb was extremely mobile, and she was not about to be caught.

There I was, chasing an uncatchable lamb around the lower pasture while in the upper pasture the rest of the flock grazed contentedly. I tried baaing like a sheep to see if she would follow me. She did, for a while, but as soon as we got out of sight of the familiar barn and the lower pasture she turned and went running back to where she had last seen the flock.

How ironic. In all the lost sheep stories I have heard, none have included the theory that the lamb was lost because the rest of the flock had moved on, and there was one that just refused to leave what was familiar. This sheep wasn't lost, but "left behind." What a world of metaphors that observation opens up.

In the end, I finally got the lamb to head down the dead end drive where the gate to my property was shut. Then, as she tried to dive back into the lower pasture, she got her head caught in the fence and I grabbed her legs. Kind of like the Jesus picture after all, but without the cliff, thank goodness.

I carried her back to the flock, and when the rest of the sheep were within sight, I set her down. This time when she called out, her mom casually called back. The lamb ran off to be reunited with her community and started nibbling at some grass, as if nothing had happened.

I, of course, began writing another "Lost Sheep" sermon.

KARMA DOG

As a pastor, I am so immersed in the church community that I can lose my perspective on what kind of community we are. Joining other communities helps me notice parallels, make comparisons, and regain perspective on what matters. The sheepdog world has been one of those "communities of perspective" for me.

As part of my preparation for a trip to Great Britain in 2011, I became a member of the International Sheep Dog Society. The ISDS is headquartered in England, and by "Sheep Dog," of course, they mean border collie. I was surprised to discover there is an application process to join the ISDS; I thought I would just pay the fee and be in. Instead, I was asked on the application if I would uphold the principles of the Society and abide by its standards in support of the working sheep dog. I said "Yes" and paid my fifty pounds. The Sheep Dog Society is something special, having been in existence for more than one hundred years. I have never thought of it as an exclusive group, but still, it was nice to be welcomed in. I felt like I was a part of something special.

My membership confirmation came in the mail with an issue of *The International Sheep Dog Society News*. I picked up the magazine and came across the following notice, right in the front: "An apology to all Irish single handlers at this year's International Trial. The sequencing of positions 4 to 15 at the Irish National was read out correctly on the trial field, and that was reported to the web site correctly. Unfortunately, the sequence was recorded wrongly and this was copied to the International Programme run order. The misplacing would have been small, but it should not have happened and we apologise."

I was impressed. This group of folks knew how to welcome someone and how to apologize too. If my church could get those two things right, we would be a long way towards creating the community we are called to be.

"There is no good flock without a good shepherd and no good shepherd without a good dog."

This old Scottish saying is the motto of the International Sheepdog Society. It evokes for me not only my life as a shepherd, but also my life as a pastor. Any pastor who remembers that Jesus is the Good Shepherd might wonder what kind of dog that shepherd had, but Scottish shepherds and I know it was a border collie.

If a person is fortunate, life will bring that person many good dogs. I have been fortunate. One of those good dogs was

Buddy. He got his nickname "Karma Dog" when he showed up at my farm down in Oregon right after I moved there from California. He was young, wild, and lost. The first few days I had him, I resisted naming him as I tried to find his owner. I was sure someone was searching for him; I called the humane society, put an ad in the paper, and waited.

In the meantime, this new dog made a pest of himself. He was completely out of control, and he was starved not only for something to eat but for attention too. Any time he saw me he would come running and jump all over me. He was not housebroken, so he pretty much had to stay outside, which added a dimension of mud to his jumping. He had the black and white tuxedo look of a Border collie, but he was bigger than any Border collie I knew, and he didn't behave like one. He chased sheep rather than herding them. No chicken was safe anywhere near him.

A week passed with no response to my ad. I began to suspect that maybe this dog was not so much lost as he was abandoned. After a month, I was pretty sure of it. Finally, I gave him a name—Buddy—hoping he would grow into it. I also began calling him my karma dog. All the other dogs that had ever lived with me had some discernible purpose. The dogs on my farm at the time Buddy showed up were working dogs, each playing their important role—as herder, guardian, and companion. Buddy didn't fit in any of those categories. Buddy was the dog the universe had given me to take care of, as a way to pay back for all the good dogs who had been a part of my life. When I moved up to Washington with my sheep and my other two dogs, Buddy came with us.

My other dogs were trained to follow commands when they rounded up sheep. "Come bye" means head out to the left, and "away to me" means go right. Training Buddy, though, seemed hopeless. I tried, not very successfully, to teach him some basic manners, and left it at that.

Then, somewhere along the way, the sheep knowledge Buddy carried inside of himself began to show. Buddy had been taking notes. He was studying what the other dogs did, and he started to trust his instincts. One night, after I had sent Lizzie for the sheep, I noticed that Buddy had gone as well, and was trailing after them just like Lizzie did. Another night, I noticed that when Lizzie missed some of the sheep that were at the top of the pasture, Buddy had kept going, and brought those sheep in all by himself. After that, if I simply said, "Bring 'em," Buddy would go out and, in his own faithful and wonderful way, bring 'em.

Buddy was a self-taught sheepdog. He did not know any of the traditional sheep dog vocabulary, but he was very good at what he did. He was so good, in fact, that he became my "go to" dog when the sheep were far away and scattered. He would go all the way out and keep going until he brought back every one. Some nights I would think I had asked too much of him. Then the sheep would appear out of the darkness, hurrying toward the barn, with Buddy following behind like the good dog he was. My "karma dog" turned out to be another gift the universe gave to me.

Buddy had a rough start in life. He even had a rough start with me. He was not the dog I thought I wanted; he was simply the dog I had. We got to know each other. We got to know more of ourselves. At the end, I was aware of a deep bond, a love that existed between the two of us. How did that happen?

I believe there is a circle of love in this world. I believe it begins with God, and it is central to the meaning of our existence. When one is willing to jump into the circle, the real adventures of life begin. That belief makes me deeply grateful for all in my life who have jumped into that circle with me, who taught me how to love by loving me.

On my Washington farm, Buddy grew old and slowed down a bit. He never lost his resilient spirit, though, and by the end of his life, he had grown completely into his name. After sixteen years, when I had to say goodbye to him, I told my friends, "Now the Good Shepherd has another good sheep dog."

———◆———

ORGANIC, SUSTAINABLE SPIRITUALITY

Farming is a spiritual practice. There is no doubt in my mind about it. The rhythm of rising early to chores, the day-in and day-out demands of the animals, without regard to season or weather, the sheer physicality of moving tons of hay from truck to barn to feeder, the quiet evenings watching over the flock as they graze their way back down to the barn, all of this is a part of the powerful connection to life that I feel whenever I let my farm and its work come deeply into my awareness. It is an instinctual sense that if I can just get outside, if I can just listen to the earth, if I can just be aware of this ordinary moment, of the animals in my care, of the ground on which I stand, my spirit will be fed.

So every spring when visitors swarm over my farm, as my two flocks meet in the spring ritual we call "Lamb Day," the seeds of the sacred are already present. I never say those words, but I trust the process. Get on a ferry; travel over water. Come to the farm; meet the animals. Stay awhile. It won't be quiet; in fact, it might be quite chaotic. It won't necessarily be relaxing. There is often the stress of a long ferry line. It might be a struggle to get everyone up and going. It can be complicated to figure out schedules and carpools and all the arrangements of getting from there to here.

Once folks arrive, we won't talk about Bible stories or reflect on deep spiritual truths. Our liturgy will be the words of our ordinary conversation, and our hymns will be the shouts and laughter of our children. We will hear them wash over us as the sound comes up from the pasture where the children are watching the lambs. The Sacred will be there. It will soak through us all on this day, whatever the day holds.

When people come to my farm, I see it through new eyes. Sometimes I spot things I should have taken care of but have stopped noticing. One year a child asked if my old farm tractor worked; it sits out in the field and I stopped noticing it years ago. "No, it needs to be fixed," I answered.

"Well, let's fix it now," he replied. "I know how to fix tractors!" If I could have found a wrench, he would have marched right out there to try.

Some folks see things I haven't seen at all. One year a child made a map of the woods after he had hiked through, and on the map, to help others find their way, he placed the following landmarks: "Dead bird #1" and "Dead bird #2."

Those landmarks weren't there the following year, but the people who helped prepare the trail for the day found some bones, and thoughtfully placed them to the side of the trail for some young adventurer to spot.

One year when there were no lambs, we hatched chicks. Chicken eggs take twenty-one days, more or less, to become actual chicks. I gathered six eggs over the course of a week.

Then, when the temperature in my incubator reached 100 degrees, I carefully placed them on the wire rack inside. When I woke up the next morning, I checked on the eggs and the incubator, and saw that the temperature had risen to 105. Oh no. I turned the thermostat down and hoped the eggs were ok.

Throughout the next week, I faithfully turned the eggs morning and night. Sometimes when I accidently bumped the incubator all the eggs would roll in a jumble. Was this bad for them? I didn't know, but I suspected so. Still, I would pick them all up again and put them back where they had been.

At the end of that first week, I candled the eggs: holding them up to a strong light to see through the shells and decide if a chick is growing inside. In spite of the fact that I carefully read and followed the candling instructions, I really couldn't tell what was going on inside the eggs. I wasn't optimistic, but for three weeks I went on faith. I just kept turning the eggs and monitoring the temperature and hoping. The day before Lamb Day was full of getting ready for the crowd to come and wondering if there would be chicks hatching the next day. Just before I went to bed, as I was checking the eggs one last time, I thought I heard a peep. My dog Mac seemed to hear it too, and looked up intently at the incubator, which he had not noticed before.

It is a strange thing to me, that chicks in eggs that are about to hatch might peep, and that those of us in the outside world might hear them. I think of eggs as a solid barrier between inside and outside, but they are actually quite permeable. Light and air and even bacteria can all get in, and the chirps the about-to-hatch chick makes can get out. Was that peep just my imagination? I waited and listened but heard nothing more. Mac went back out to the other room. I went to bed, hoping there would be at least one chick hatching the next day, and hoping it would hatch when all the families were here.

The next morning when I went down to make the final preparations for the crowd about to arrive, I checked the incubator again, of course. As I looked in, I saw that one of the eggs had a large crack in it, and I could see movement inside. I was surprised by how excited I was. When the first cars arrived with my visitors, I ran down to the parking area and said, "An egg is hatching! Come watch it!" Then I added, "Oh yeah, and welcome to the farm." I hurried those first guests back to the house and we all looked in the incubator. There we saw a little, wet, black chick, newly hatched and just stretching out from an egg-shaped curl to a chick-shaped stand. A miracle.

Over the course of the next six hours, as folks came and went, four more of the eggs hatched. Children would gather around to look for a bit, and then leave. It was mostly we adults who kept coming back to watch, as one more egg began to rock and then crack to reveal the hard-working hatchling inside. I was riveted and delighted by the sight. Each chick, after hatching, would lie there awhile exhausted. I would wonder if it was going to be ok. Then it would shudder and twitch and stand and, over the course of about an hour, dry out and fluff up and be just fine.

I was surprised at how thrilling all of this was. That the eggs hatched. That they hatched right at the time I had hoped. That I ended up with five delightful chicks, each one different, from yellow to brown striped to black. That I got to share this new-life vigil with my congregation.

The fifth chick came out just before the last visitors left, and, as it turned out, that was the last egg to hatch. I gave the sixth egg three more days but it never moved and never peeped. Finally I unplugged the incubator, and gave the egg a semi-dignified burial by throwing it in the blackberry bushes where the dogs couldn't get it. The five chicks that hatched became a part of my third flock, the chicken one, and gave me eggs for many years after that.

The following year I tried to repeat the experience. Once again I put six eggs in the incubator and waited. That year, however, none of the eggs hatched during Lamb Day. It was only after everyone had left that I heard peeping coming from the incubator sitting on the washing machine. I looked into the incubator to see a brand-new chick, with egg shell pieces scattered all around her. She had arrived about two hours too late to be witnessed by anyone but me. I took her out and put her under the heat lamp. She was the only chick who hatched out of those six eggs.

So every spring I say to the congregation, "Come. Be here. Have fun." I know they will go home renewed. It's an organic, sustainable spirituality at work. Francis of Assisi is reported to have said, "Preach the gospel at all times. If necessary, use words." It is incarnation, after all—Word-Become-Flesh, God-with-Us—that is at the heart of our faith.

The day after Lamb Day, when I am scheduled to preach, I manage to work up a sermon. The truth, though, is that I am sure it is the out-in-the-sun connection-beyond-words farm sermons that the congregation will remember.

———◆———

Church Time

ORDINARY TIME

———◆———

———◆———

Farm Time

MAY-NOVEMBER

THE GIFT OF ORDINARY TIME

As cute as tiny lambs are, and as exciting as lambing time is, it only takes me one full night of sleep to remember that I like Ordinary Time. I like the name of it, the feel of it, and the imagery it calls to mind. In the church calendar, Ordinary Time is the span of days between Pentecost and Advent, such a long season that we easily lose count of the days. ("Ordinary" relates to "ordinal," meaning ordered or sequenced.) Ordinary Time keeps the long days in order. Ordinary Time is also scripturally uneventful: Jesus is not being born or baptized, he is not being arrested or executed, we are not remembering his death or his resurrection. We are simply living our lives in the world as Christians.

On the farm, there are no heavy demands on any of the flock. The rams are in their bachelor pen, relaxed and undistracted from their grazing. The ewes are not growing lambs or birthing them. Most of the lambs are weaned or close to it, and big enough now to almost be sheep themselves. Each creature simply gets on with the daily tasks of eating and sleeping and eating again. My own days are relaxed as well. The pasture is full of grass, the barn is full of hay, and the sun is keeping us all warm.

My sister told me that (nonchurch) ordinary time is one of the things she misses the most, now that her children are grown and gone. "Sitting together at the breakfast table, checking in at night, telling all the little details of the day, reading the paper in the family room while they are working at the computer. I look back now," she said, "and know those were some of the most precious times we had."

Life is made up of many extraordinary moments and milestones: a wedding, the birth of a child, a graduation. Still, it is in ordinary time that we ultimately shape our lives: how we live out those wedding vows, how we love the child who is born, how we apply what we've learned to each day.

One of the earliest church events I hosted at my farm was a sleepover with fifth graders. In preparation for their arrival, I printed out our schedule on a large poster. For the morning activities, at 7:00 AM I listed "Chores (Optional)." Of course, chores are not optional for me, but for that group of kids, they were. Chores usually aren't particularly exciting, or stimulating, or daring, and I was not going to add to my list of chores, "Wake up sleepy fifth graders and take them, protesting, out to work around the farm." As soon as the fifth graders saw the schedule, though, they said enthusiastically, "Chores! We get to do chores?!!" The following morning, they got up early and very conscientiously did chores.

The thing about chores is that—while they are regular, maintenance things we have to do—in each chore, in each moment, there is wondrous possibility. God often shows up in the ordinary. God shows up in the chores. That is true at my church as well; there is something very steadying about the regular rhythm of Bible study, pastoral visits, sermon preparation, and even meetings, week after week. I am always grateful for the work I am called to do. My faithfulness in the everyday ordinary times prepares me for those extraordinary moments of faithfulness that come without regard to calendar or liturgical season. Ordinary Time is the best season for learning that balance. In Ordinary Time, we get to do chores.

PSALM 23

When I was in seminary many years ago, the little book called *A Shepherd Looks at the 23rd Psalm,* by Phillip Keller, was popular. Keller was a shepherd in British Columbia and used his observations about sheep and shepherds to speak authoritatively about the metaphors of this well-loved psalm of faith.

Many sermons I heard on Psalm 23 in those days would reference the book and remind us that sheep are stupid and stubborn creatures that need constant guidance, vigilant supervision, and strict boundaries to avoid death either by predator or by their slow-minded wandering in the fatal direction of some cliff. "Sheep just follow the flock," the book told us.

So preachers would warn the sheep-like humans of their own flock to beware those who might lead us astray by way of peer pressure or secular values.

Once I became a shepherd, I took a second look at that book. As I reread it, I found myself both appalled and amused.

In my experience, sheep are not stupid creatures. They are quite wise when it comes to the ways of a sheep and generally thrive living within those ways. If someone took a magic wand and turned me (or you) into a sheep, and we tried to live as sheep with our own independent twenty-first-century mindset, we would not last long. Old shepherds have told me more than once: if I conclude that my sheep are stubborn, I should probably take a good look at my own hard-headedness.

Here's where I think that the shepherd of that old book went wrong. When Keller looked at the 23rd Psalm, he began not with the sheep but with his own theology. In that framework, he viewed humans as totally depraved with no good in us, simply at the mercies of evil until Christ the Good Shepherd rescues us, always prone to wander off from God's goodness. Keller then applied the metaphor backwards. If humans are dumb, then the sheep of Psalm 23 must be dumb too. If humans are bound to get life wrong, then sheep too must be helpless without the strong guidance of a shepherd. The more we acknowledge our stupid sheepiness, Keller concluded, the more God can work with us to help us.

Now that I have kept sheep for so many years, all my assumptions about the biblical imagery of sheep and shepherd have been stretched and challenged. I read the worn and familiar phrases of this most beloved psalm with new perspective. Consider, for example, the opening description of sheep lying down in green pastures, with still waters nearby. For a shepherd, there is no finer sight than the flock at rest in the midst of abundance. It is a profound image of contentment. The sheep are neither hungry (or they'd be up and eating) nor alarmed (or they'd be fleeing). They are satisfied and safe. Such a vision restores and shepherd's soul.

So I push back on Keller's conclusions, having shepherded people and sheep alike that are as curious as they are stubborn. Metaphorically and actually, sheep reflect God's beautiful life in the world. The more I open myself to noticing it, the more I am transformed to hold an inclusive and celebratory understanding of my Christian faith. There is a sacredness in all of life. God's goodness is found everywhere. And sheep are not dumb.

At a weekly Bible study with preaching colleagues, I came prepared to counter Keller's book as we contemplated, "The Lord is my shepherd . . ." When we sat down with the psalm, I jumped right in. "Whatever you do, don't say sheep are dumb!"

My colleague Amy looked at me in a surprised way and said, "Why on earth would I say that sheep are dumb?"

"Well, haven't you ever read that book, *A Shepherd Looks at the 23rd Psalm*?" I asked.

"Never heard of it," she said.

EWELOGY

It was on a Monday night about ten years ago that I arrived home to my farm after a full day of work at my Seattle church and found that my old ewe Silver had died. Silver was one of the first sheep I ever owned. She was already five years old when she came to my farm in Oregon, and had it not been for a sheep tragedy, she would not have come at all.

I became a shepherd when I moved from California to Oregon. I purchased my first four sheep from a shepherd who had hundreds. Ruth Ann kept Romneys, a breed from a wet part of England; they do well in the wet Pacific Northwest. Ruth Ann sold me three ewes, and one came with a lamb.

I was thrilled to bring them home in my pickup truck. Once they were out in the pasture, I watched them all afternoon and into the evening as they grazed. When they finally bedded down out there, I went inside and bedded down too. The next morning when I got up and ran out to check on them, three of the four sheep, including the lamb, were dead.

I was devastated. I had been a shepherd less than twenty-four hours, and I had just been taught the hardest lesson shepherds have to learn. The flock is vulnerable. The flock is fragile. In a world of predators, the flock is prey.

I called the county extension service to report the loss and see if they could help me figure out what happened. The agent came out, looked around and said it was probably young coyotes. Coyotes attack the back legs, while cougars go for the shoulders and neck, he explained. Had it been dogs, I would have lost all four, because dogs "attacks" are play; they don't stop until they've played with everyone, and everyone has stopped playing back. Coyotes typically kill only what they eat. Usually all you find after coyotes visit your flock are a few pieces of their dinner. In this case, though, they had taken down three and only eaten a bit of each one, which made the agent think they were young coyotes accompanied by an older teacher.

It was a harsh education in the realities of country life. My heart broke like a city girl's, but at that same moment, I think my shepherd's heart began to beat. I went to work. I buried the remains of the three dead sheep and took the lone survivor back to the farm she came from. Then I measured the open sides of the pole barn on my property and contacted a local lumber mill to order custom-cut cedar siding. A barn that is too snug is not good for sheep; they need good air circulation, and they can't stay healthy if they're too hot.

In two weeks, I had an enclosed area, not too snug and not too hot, that would be a safe place for my new flock to spend each night. I researched "predator control" and eventually acquired two gifted guardian dogs—Luke and Turk—to live with the flock day and night and keep the coyotes away. Until Luke and Turk arrived, though, the barn would have to do.

With everything ready, I got four more sheep. Silver was one of those four—in fact, the oldest of the four—and I got her at a discount because of that. Ruth Ann, my sheep supplier, was fond of her, which was why Silver had a name and why Ruth Ann said to me, "All I ask is that she not be a cull." She was asking me to keep Silver for life.

I was new to farming. What did I know about how sheep multiply, and how you can't keep them all? What did I know about how good shepherds have to decide regularly which sheep stay and which ones move on—usually based on whether they are good mothers that produce good lambs? I said OK.

A few years later, when I chose which sheep to take with me from Oregon to Washington to begin my ministry at a Seattle church and my farm life on Whidbey Island, Silver was the first one picked. She was a very good mother who regularly had twins, and she was exceptionally attentive to her lambs. Her wool was a beautiful soft gray. One year my sister found someone to spin it and, to my surprise and delight, knitted me a vest for Christmas.

It was on a Friday, years later, when I found Silver under the barn, where the raised foundation provides a dark and cool refuge. She was in labor and clearly having a hard time of it. I tried to coax her out, but she was lying on her side and wouldn't get up, so I crawled to her and discovered that the lamb inside her was stuck. Lambs are supposed to dive into the world, two front legs forward, with their nose tucked snugly between. One of this lamb's front legs, however, was folded back. The leg had to be brought around before Silver could deliver.

As I went up to the house to get some hot water, rags, and disinfectant, my phone rang. One of my parishioners had passed away and it was his wife calling. Could I come?

Sometimes choices come down to figuring out which crisis needs the most immediate attention. Clearly a pastor needed to be there. Just as clearly, if I left Silver under the barn, she and her lamb would die. Quickly I came to a hard decision. I had walked with this parishioner and his wife through the illness that had ultimately claimed him. I wanted to be there, but I couldn't leave the farm.

Promising to call her right back, I hung up and phoned my colleague Don. Could he make this pastoral visit in my stead? Yes, he could. I called the parishioner back and explained that I couldn't be there for at least three hours, but Don could come immediately. I crawled back under the barn as Don went to comfort a grieving family.

There I was, scrubbing my arm just like I had read in the James Herriot books, just like I was taught by the folks at the extension "lamb school" I had attended. I reached in to find the lamb and worked my fingers across the tiny shoulder and down along the leg that was back, until I had hold of the little hoof. Grasping it firmly, I gently pulled the leg around. It had to be uncomfortable for Silver, but she was patient. With the leg finally in the right position, the lamb slipped out—a big, beautiful ram lamb. Silver was relieved and energized. As I put the lamb by her nose, she sniffed him and began to clean him off.

"When you have to intervene in a birth," they taught me in lamb school, "always check for a second lamb." I scrubbed up again, reached back in, and found the second lamb, way back. Its legs and head were positioned perfectly, and as I pulled, it came easily into the world. A little ewe. Wonderful.

One week later, Don and I conducted the memorial service for our parishioner.

Eventually I took Silver out of the lambing rotation. She became a retired lady, the matriarch of the flock. For several years, I kept thinking she wouldn't make it through the winter, but she kept surprising me.

Then, as winter approached that final year, Silver started falling often. Several times that autumn, I came home to find her lying on her side, like she did that day under the barn. Now, however, it was because she couldn't get up on her own, and I had to help. Every time she fell, it was harder for her to rise.

She was down again one Monday morning, and nothing I did helped. So I stroked her nose and told her what a good ewe she was. I held her head up, and gave her a little alfalfa, which she ate eagerly. Then I set her head back down. She seemed at rest. She was still there in the evening when I got home. Sometime during the day, Silver had died.

I buried her on the farm, and I recited for her the William Blake poem I recite for all my lambs:

Little Lamb, who made thee?
Dost thou know who made thee?
Gave thee life and bid thee feed,
By the stream and o'er the mead;
Gave thee clothing of delight,
Softest clothing, woolly, bright;
Gave thee such a tender voice,
Making all the vales rejoice!
Little Lamb, who made thee?
Dost thou know who made thee?
Little lamb, I'll tell thee,
Little lamb, I'll tell thee.
He is called by thy name,
For He calls Himself a Lamb:
He is meek and He is mild,
He became a little child:
I a child and thou a lamb,
We are called by His name.
Little lamb, God bless thee!
Little lamb God bless thee![3]

---

3. Public domain.

SHEEPDOG SENSEI

"Come bye," I call to Rose, and she takes the command, sweeps left and clockwise to gather the sheep. Only I didn't want her to sweep left; I wanted her to move right. I have given the wrong command. "Away to me," I correct myself, asking her to change direction. She looks at me briefly and keeps going left. "Lie down, hey, away to me, no!" The commands and corrections are pouring out of me now, each one contradicting the other as I feel myself becoming more tense. With the flurry of commands, I have left Rose confused and on her own out there with the sheep.

I am learning to move sheep with a talented, trained and experienced sheepdog. I have moved sheep with not very highly trained dogs, with a grain bucket, and sometimes with brute force. None of those styles is particularly reliable or effective. I have never partnered with a dog like Rose. She is very good. She is also, thank goodness, forgiving.

The story of how Rose has come to be with me is one of generosity and grace. My friend Susan had been helping me train my dogs to a "sheepdog trial" level of work, but things were not going very well. "We have to find Catherine an experienced dog to teach her how to work." Susan was talking with Patrick Shannahan, a top dog handler who had come to her farm to give lessons. I had signed up for one with my young dog Annie. Annie had been struggling with her sheep lessons and I, inexperienced as I was, could not help her. Susan thought I needed lessons too, from an experienced dog.

"Maybe we can find Catherine a trial dog who is ready to retire." Susan said to Patrick.

"Let me think about it," he answered. Later, after working a few more dogs who were also there for lessons, Patrick walked back over to us. "I'll let her borrow Rose," he said.

"That could work," Susan said, and then, when Patrick had walked away, looked at me and added, "Wow." Patrick Shannahan, one of the top handlers in the world, had just offered me, a beginner, one of his retired dogs. Rose had run in competition, had helped with Patrick's clinics, and was his "go to" chore dog for work on his Idaho sheep farm. In my mind, it was as if a top race car driver had handed me the keys to the Ferrari he wasn't racing with just now.

Once Rose arrived on my farm, I began to call her my Sheepdog Sensei. I worked her on Susan's sheep, and I tried her out on mine as well. She was responsive, respectful, and very, very good. She was teaching me, and as it turns out, she was teaching my sheep too, what it means to work with a dog who knows what she's doing.

Working sheep with a teammate presents its own set of challenges. I have to remember that she is there. I am so accustomed to doing the work on my own that I automatically respond to the sheep independently of this good dog. But she is right there and eager to work. I no longer have to do it on my own. I also show my "beginner partner" status when I over-command. "She knows what to do," Susan reminds me. "Keep your eyes on the sheep, not on the dog. Trust her." So I relax and let Rose do her part of our work.

In my Seattle congregation, we are all about team. Instead of one person at the top of a staffing hierarchy, we have a Leadership Team of three pastors and a church administrator to provide guidance and support. Church members team with pastors and staff as we find ways to move forward in our spiritual work. "Remember to look for your teammates," one of my colleagues is fond of saying. From this congregation I have learned a great deal about team.

But clearly, I still have a lot to learn.

With sheep and dogs, the feedback regarding my teaming skills is immediate and very evident. I can see the benefits of good partnering, as well as the effects of my forgetfulness or my micromanagement right away. With my congregational teammates, feedback is more subtle and less swift. But Rose reminds me of the importance and even the joy of partnership. She helps me tone down my tendency to be controlling and to remember to look for my partners when the pressure rises and I feel myself beginning to tense up. I am not in this alone.

ANIMAL HUNGER

Sheep test fences. That is a fact of farm life that keeps a farmer on her toes. Just like a bike rider has to keep moving forward to keep her balance, a farmer has to build and check fences to manage stock.

Summer is the time of the year when fence testing is at its most intense. The grass has been grazed out or dried out. The hay that looked good in the winter does not look as tasty after the green spring diet that has been the mainstay of the flock for the last few months. Casual fences that have kept them on the farm when grass was plentiful are no match for my determined sheep in the summer.

So it was that several years ago I got a call from my neighbor up the road that my sheep were out. "I saw them headed over to our new neighbors' place," she reported. Animal hunger can be a powerful force, and the flock had found its way out and over to greener pastures.

My new neighbors were away for the weekend, and I was also away from home. It was the end of our week-long church camp. I suppose that when the shepherd's away, the sheep will play. I called my sheep-sitter Lori and left a message. "Escaped sheep, last seen heading over to John and Virginia's.

Could you check on them?" By the time Lori got there, the sheep had come back home. They looked up at her innocently as if to say, "Who, us?"

The evidence of their wanderings, though, was everywhere. My neighbors, who were turning their farm into an equestrian center, had just remodeled their barn and reseeded their pasture. Now their lovely, clean barn had been invaded and used as a bathroom. Yes, that happens to barns, but really, don't you want it to be *your* animals who get to use your new barn first?

The neighbors had cameras on their property, placed carefully in the hopes of catching photos of wild animals that might wander through. Even if my sheep tried to blame some rogue deer for the mess they made of the place, there was photographic evidence. The pictures showed them relaxing in the shade of the barn, wandering through the stalls, and grazing on the reseeded pasture. There was even a picture of my guardian dog Giacco at the party.

When my neighbors and I returned to our homes, we inspected the damage. The neighbors were gracious about it, and I did what I could to clean things up.

As a result of their wanderings, my sheep ended up in confinement in the lower, well-fenced pasture. They lost their freedom, they were put on hay rations, and they complained about it all. I tried to tell them that the grass is just about gone anyway, but they still griped. As if to demonstrate her dissatisfaction, one of the ewes got her head caught when she stuck it through the pasture fence to grab some little bite of something on the other side. I had to cut the fence to free her.

Sheep, like all of us, don't necessarily want to eat what is right in front of them. They have some strong inclinations to wander for the sake of their appetites. A friend of mine once suggested that the lost sheep in Jesus' parable, for which the shepherd went searching, likely nibbled herself away from the rest of the flock without even knowing what she was doing. From what I know of sheep, I don't imagine nibbling. I believe she stepped out boldly and would not be deterred in her wandering. And yes, it probably involved food.

LATE-NIGHT RADIO RETREAT

It is late evening on the farm, and I am out rounding up sheep. This is a common exercise for me in the fall, when the daylight is short, workdays are long, and my hungry sheep wander far looking for grass. Fall is in the middle of the season that church folks call "Ordinary Time." This is the longest liturgical season of the year, when nothing particularly notable (from a liturgical point of view) is happening. No Christmas. No Easter. Not even Pentecost. Just the ordinary stuff of day-to-day living. On the farm, the drama and immediacy of lambing is long past. The cute little lambs are now half-grown sheep.

Ordinary Time can feel like an "in-between" time, a time to get through until we get to the good stuff. However, it doesn't take much of a deeper look to realize that day-to-day is what reveals the reality of any life, whether it be a life of faith or a life of shepherding. In Ordinary Time, I remember what it means to be an everyday shepherd. Today, after a full day of pastoral visits, phone calls, and meetings at the church, being a shepherd includes tracking down my farm flock in the dark.

I hike to the pasture at the top of my property, with my smart phone keeping me company. I carry a phone when I do chores alone on the farm, so I can call for help if I get myself in over my head. Tonight I am streaming our local public radio station. There in the dark, with a quarter moon in the sky and the sheep hiding up the hill, I hear two gentle southern accents. The first one I recognize immediately. It is Bill Moyers, host of the PBS series "Moyers and Company." I enjoy listening to his sweet Texas-tinged drawl. The second voice also has a soft southern cadence. It is familiar, but I can't place it. I keep listening.

They are talking about family. "It is a sacrament, and something of a responsibility, to love someone," says the voice I can't place. His words are so wise, I strain to figure out who he is, hoping Bill might say his name.

They talk a bit about commitment, and then they shift to talking about faith. Bill remarks, "You still consider yourself a Christian."

"I still consider myself a person who takes the Gospels very seriously." Who is this other person answering Bill's question?

Then Bill says, "Read your own poem." and the man begins to recite. "The Peace of Wild Things," he announces.

> *When despair for the world grows in me,*
> *and I wake in the night at the least sound*
> *in fear of what my life and my children's life may be,*
> *I go and lie down where the wood drake*
> *rests in his beauty on the water, and the great heron feeds.*
> *I come into the peace of wild things...*[4]

Of course! I am listening to Wendell Berry, talking with Bill about the sacred earth, about justice, about faith. Suddenly I don't care if I find the sheep soon or not. I am transfixed.

The wisdom keeps coming. "The whole thing is holy," Wendell says, talking about life and the earth and all of creation. "There are no sacred and unsacred places; there are only sacred and desecrated places."

The talk turns to Wendell's Kentucky farm. "Ask the land what it needs. Don't try to impose your will on the land, but be patient. To be patient in an emergency is a terrible trial. But it is what we need now."

---

4. *The Selected Poems of Wendell Berry* (Counterpoint, 1999), 30. Reprinted by permission of Counterpoint Press.

"Do you have hope?" Bill asks, and Wendell answers with another reading.

> *The young ask the old to hope.*
> *What will you tell them?*
> *Tell them at least what you say to yourself.*
>
> *Because we have not made our lives to fit*
> *Our places, the forests are ruined, the fields eroded*
> *The mountains overturned. Hope*
> *Then to belong to your place by your own knowledge*
> *Of what it is that no other place is, and by*
> *Your caring for it as you care for no other place . . .*
> *Find your hope then, on the ground under your feet.*
> *Your hope of Heaven, let it rest on the ground*
> *Underfoot . . .*[5]

Here I am, standing in the upper pasture of a farm I call my own, with land I call my own underfoot. For years now I have been trying to know this place, to ask the land what it needs, to ask the creatures what they need, and to listen. I realize Wendell has given me words for listening to my other flock, too, those folks in Seattle. In the city, in my commitment to the needs of the people, I strive to be still and listen.

---

5. Wendell Berry, *Leavings* (Counterpoint, 2010), 91. Reprinted by permission of Counterpoint Press.

I find my hope in caring for my congregation and in the work that is right in front of me to do.

As the interview ends, I look up and there are the sheep, standing close by, as if they've come over to listen to Wendell and Bill too. Without planning to, I have been on a half-hour retreat. I feel grounded and renewed.

The sheep and I walk back to the barn, quiet in our individual reflections, and more hopeful than any of us have been for a while.

PROPHET DOG, PASTOR DOG

In the congregation I serve, my ministry focuses on two areas: our love and justice ministry and our parish life ministry. The church's love and justice ministry engages in social action, caring for those on the margins and pushing to change the structures that marginalize anyone. I love that work. It is part of what keeps my ministry vital and alive. The parish life ministry, on the other hand, focuses on the care we give one another in the church, keeping an eye on one another, making sure folks are connected and cared for. I love this work too. It helps me stay in touch with the realities of life and faith within me.

These two areas of my ministry require opposite energies: challenging and reassuring people, or, as is often said among

Christian ministers, "comforting the afflicted and afflicting the comfortable."

In other words, I am called to be a pastor and a prophet.

What is true in my ministry is true on my farm as well. Currently, four dogs help my work there. Three are border collies. The fourth is my guardian dog, Giaco. Giaco is a Maremma, a type of livestock guardian dog bred to work in the Maremma section of the Italian Alps, guarding large flocks from predators. Because he is Italian, Giaco is named after the Italian composer Giacomo Puccini, as well as the racehorse Giacomo, who won the 2005 Kentucky Derby as a long shot.

Giaco the dog is himself as refined as an opera singer and as raffish as a racehorse. He came to me when he got fired from his previous job, guarding poultry on a farm in eastern Washington. Turns out he has a taste for chicken. On my farm, the chickens are already in "protective custody" because my border collies think of them as fun squeaky toys. My chickens spend their days in an enclosed yard and their nights in a closed coop for their own safety.

A lot of people call Giaco a guard dog. Guardian, though, is the more accurate term. While he can intimidate predators, his presence actually creates more calm than it does fear. Maremmas are like big strong sheep to the sheep. From a distance, Maremmas' fluffy white coats help them blend right in with the flock. If a sheep is in trouble, the guardian dog will stay right there with it. When a lamb is born, the guardian dog will lie down nearby to make sure everything is ok. When the guardian dog shows up, everyone relaxes. These dogs are so calm that—despite their towering size—they are ideal for helping anxious kids get over their fear of dogs.

My border collies have a job that is exactly the opposite of Giaco's. Maremmas reassure sheep. Border collies move them. When Giaco shows up, the sheep simply think, "Oh, it's you," and go back to their grazing. When the border collies show up, the sheep go on instant alert and move away as fast as possible.

In other words, border collies afflict the comfortable and Maremmas comfort the afflicted.

On the farm, it takes two kinds of dogs to do what we ministers are asked to do on a regular basis. We hold in tension the task of caring for people right where they are and the task of taking them somewhere new. The truth is, as opposite as the role of pastor and the role of prophet feel, they are just two dimensions of the same work. We all need to be comforted in our lives. We need those places where we are safe to be who we are, where there is help if we get in trouble, where there is a strong presence that holds what we cannot hold by ourselves. We all need to be challenged as well. We need to be moved from where we are settled to the better place God has in mind for the whole world. The news provides a regular reminder that we cannot stay where we are. Thank God something more is calling us forward.

I watch my dogs play together, each confident that they can do what they were meant to do, and I see those aspects of my own call. There is so much work in the world to do, so many things that need to change—in us and for us—for our world to become a world of peace and reconciling love. I pray that I can learn how to welcome each part of my call, to honor each dimension of my work. Maybe I can even find ways to let them play together as well.

COUNTING SHEEP

It is Monday and I am doing my morning chores when I notice there is one sheep missing from the feed trough in the ram pen. This is never good news. It is late fall, the time of year when I add ewes to the ram pen with a vision for new lambs in the spring. When I realize my breeding flock is one sheep short, I am worried.

Glancing around the pen, which is rather large and full of bushy vegetation, I finally spot the downed sheep and go to see what is wrong. As I get closer, my heart sinks. It is the ram, and he is not moving. The ground around him is churned up, as if he had been struggling. I think he is probably dead.

Then he moves just a bit. He looks pretty close to gone, but at least he is alive. I grab hay from the feeder where the rest of the sheep are chomping away, scoop water from the trough into a small bucket, and go to figure out what is wrong.

At his side, I spot the problem. His back leg is tangled in some wire, and he has become trapped when the wire snagged in a log. He had gone down, and after struggling a while, had given up. I grab his leg and begin to untangle the wire. The ewes turn from the feeder and become interested in what I am doing. I have never seen sheep leave their feed to gather around a sheep in trouble. But there they are, like a prayer circle, watching closely to see what will happen next.

Finally the ram's foot is free, but he just remains on his side. I roll him onto his chest, and as he begins to get his feet under him, I continue to prop him up. With all the ewes looking on intently, he manages to stand. He staggers and looks like he might go down again but regains his balance. I bring the water and hay closer to him; he has to be thirsty and hungry after such an ordeal. Instead he immediately turns to the ewes and begins to follow one around. Water and food are not on his mind after being so close to the end.

I laugh all the way back to the house.

Counting sheep, and gathering around the lost or troubled ones, is more complicated work with my Seattle flock. Unlike my Whidbey flock, these folks come and go, according to their own schedules and needs. They get to decide on their own when they are in and when they are out. Sometimes they tell the shepherds, and sometimes they don't.

There are a variety of ways I try to keep track of the Seattle flock, kind of like the way I count my sheep in the mornings at the trough. We count the Seattle flock on Sunday mornings. The ushers take a head count during worship, and we also pass "welcome sheets" for people to write their names on. It never ceases to amuse me that the "usher count" and the "sign in" count, in all the years I've been at the church, have never been the same. The flock count is low if the ushers count at the beginning of worship when the place is just half full. If the "welcome sheets" are passed while families step out to settle the preschoolers in their classes, names are missed from the sheets.

The problem with these ever-changing numbers, of course, is that in a church community, like in any flock, it is critically important for us to keep track of each other. Sometimes a sheep has just wandered off and will come home in due time, but sometimes a sheep is in real trouble. Without a good count (or a sheep "baaing" very loudly), the shepherd may not know.

In my Seattle flock we keep track of each other in ways beyond the Sunday count. Every September members call one another to check in. Some have been away on vacation, some have been active in summer sports, some have been in the mountains or at the beach, and many have been in worship every week. We try to be sure everyone is contacted, because we know that maybe some have gotten lost or hurt and need a shepherd to come looking.

In this, my Seattle flock has an advantage over my Whidbey one. My Whidbey sheep can't count, so it is only the shepherd who misses the lost sheep. But in Seattle, we can all keep track of each other; any one of us might know when another is missing or having a hard time.

Paying attention to each one, and to one another, is a powerful life force. I am glad for every count that draws us close.

LOST AND FOUND DOG

This is one of those stories where I want to tell the end first. Annie, my border collie, is curled safe and warm in her bed as I write. She is well, and content, and presumably dreaming whatever sweet dreams come to sheepdogs.

But when Annie was a puppy, she went missing. It was on a Sunday, and I had left the farm for Seattle before the sun was up. When I finally made it home after dark, Annie was nowhere to be found. Mac, my other border collie, was right there at the gate to greet me. Giaco, my guardian dog and Annie's best friend, was up by the house, keeping his watchful eye on everything. Annie, though, was missing. I called her. Nothing. I called again. Still nothing. A tinge of fear began to rise in my chest. Where was my puppy?

I had been keeping Annie and Mac in a roomy, enclosed garden area right off my front porch where they could be safe during the day. However, Annie had found a way out of that space. I got the whistle out and blew the recall I have taught all my dogs, Annie didn't come. I took the other dogs with me and walked the trail through the woods, blowing the whistle and calling Annie's name. The other dogs ran in circles, coming each time they heard the recall, then running off through the undergrowth to explore. Neither of them seemed upset that one dog was missing. Neither of them seemed to be leading me anywhere Annie might be.

My mind played all kinds of "what if" games. "What if she is trapped somewhere? What if the coyotes got her? What if she is out on the road? What if someone has taken her? What if she needs me and I can't get to her? What if I never find her?" For every question, I tried to give myself a reassuring answer. If Annie was trapped, I would hear her barking. Giaco the guardian dog would never let coyotes near his best friend. I had just come up the road; if she was out there I would have seen her.

Anyone who has ever searched for a lost dog knows, however, it is not the head one has to answer to. It is the heart. After an hour of no pup, my heart was broken. When I called my friend Lori to join me in the search, I could not hold back my tears.

"Annie's missing," I told her through sobs.

"I'll be right there," she answered.

Lori's presence calmed me a bit. I could not call the neighbors without crying, so Lori called them for me. Only once did Lori cry too, when a kind neighbor said, "I know what it means to lose a dog."

We searched and called until it was dark. Finally, Lori headed home, back to her kids who were waiting to hear word. "I'm sure she'll show up in the morning," she said as she left. Then there was nothing else for me to do but to go to bed. Outside it was raining, and every time I thought I heard a noise, I checked the porch to see if Annie was back. No.

In the morning, the house felt empty. Yes, Mac was there, but Annie's crate was unused, and as I did my chores, only two dogs did them with me. Before I left for work, I called the local vets and the Whidbey Animals' Improvement Foundation (WAIF) and left word of my missing dog. In each case, I cried as I said the words. In each case, people on the other end of the line were kind. But no, they hadn't received any inquiries from someone who had found a dog. Then it was time to leave the farm for work. How could I go, when Annie could be anywhere? But there was nothing more I could do in that moment, and I wanted to be with my community of care.

As I stood by the gate, preparing to leave, my broken-open heart flooded with pain, feeling overwhelmed by the world's lostness in addition to my pup's. Two weeks earlier, I had preached a sermon on Jesus' parable of the lost sheep. I had talked with confidence about how home finds us even when we can't find our way home. Now here I was, wondering how to believe in homecoming for me and my dog. If home couldn't even find a little black and white border collie, what about all the other places in this broken world where there is such a deep need for home?

I reached in my pocket for my key, and my hand touched a stone that I carried from the sacred Scottish island of Iona. What I wanted in that moment was a God who would reach down and fix things, who would bring Annie home. Instead the stone reminded me that God was present, solid as a rock, no matter what might come next for me and for Annie. I was not alone. The reminder did not take away the pain or the tears. It did not make me less afraid. But deep within, I was comforted to remember the depth and breadth and length of God's love.

When I arrived at work my colleagues surrounded me with prayers and hugs and food. They were gentle as I cried through meetings, kind when I numbly sat there, and compassionate when I headed home early to post "Lost Dog" posters in my neighborhood.

As I was finishing up, my phone rang. It was Lori, calling from the office of a Whidbey vet where she works. At the end of the workday, a man had come in. "I've got a stray dog here," he said, "and I want to see if it has a microchip." Lori had looked over the counter. "That's Annie!"

I cried as I texted my family, friends, and colleagues: "Found! Fine! Amen!" Then I rushed over to get that puppy home. Annie was nonchalant about everything, seeming confident that she knew where she had been was the whole time.

So now Annie is curled safe and warm in her bed. Outside, it looks like all has returned to where it was before. For me and my broken-open heart, though, this new reminder of the vulnerability of life remains. I know that such stories do not always end well. The lost is not always found. I am freshly aware of how precious comfort is in times of fear, and of how prayer can hold me when I have no words to pray.

APPLE DAYS

In the fall, I invite my Seattle flock to "Apple Day" On the farm. We pick apples from the trees someone before me planted in thoughtful variety and abundance, and make cider from a press donated by a couple in our congregation. We walk through the woods, check in with the sheep that have grown since Lamb Day, and have rambunctious fun. All together, we enjoy the beauty of autumn. Through the years, Apple Day has become something of a "Two Flock" institution. When the farm and the weather cooperate, and the apples are perfectly ripe, and the cider press is working, we always have an enjoyable time.

But one year, Whidbey Island was hit by tent caterpillars. The spring outbreak was so bad that trees were bare all across the south end of the island. I officiated an outdoor wedding where the hosts spent the day before the ceremony washing caterpillars off the side of their house. The next day couple spoke their vows quickly, before another wave of bugs had a chance to crawl back up and cover the house again. They were everywhere.

On my farm, the caterpillars climbed into every apple tree. They chewed the leaves down to the branch, and left my orchard looking dead. I feared the trees would never bear fruit again. The prospects for Apple Day that fall seemed a bit grim. Without apples to wash and cut and crush and juice, what would we do?

Apple Day was on my mind when I went to a neighborhood picnic of Whidbey Island locals. The event had hot dogs, coleslaw, bluegrass music, and face painting . . . and a huge slingshot-looking device set up on the baseball diamond. Kids put a squash in the sling, pulled it back with all their might, and then let go. The squash—zucchini or butternut or whatever the child had brought—would fly out across the infield, beyond second base, and into center field.

That was it. Nothing fancy. Nothing electronic. Nothing particularly productive. Just stuff soaring out onto a field. Kids were lined up waiting for a chance to fling their own little hunk of vegetable. They experimented with angle and tension, adjusting everything until they thought the moment was just right, trying to get each squash to go out farther than the previous one. Watching the kids, I thought again about Apple Day. It was scheduled for the day after Halloween. What if we had a slingshot there for pumpkins?

I quickly got a beginner's education in flinging stuff. There is a difference between a sling shot, a catapult, and something I had never heard of: a trebuchet. A sling shot is a pull-back-and-let-go kind of thing. A catapult is a pull-down-and-fling-up kind of thing. But a trebuchet is a wonderful hybrid of pull-down, sling-back, fling-out kind of thing. Ed, our congregation's go-to engineer, had one and agreed to bring it to the farm.

On Apple Day, Ed arrived with all the pieces and parts. Some mechanically minded folks joined in the fun of putting the contraption together. A van full of youth arrived with pumpkins. Families came with left over jack-o-lanterns from the night before. One parishioner who couldn't make it herself sent two pumpkins to be chucked. Soon there was a pile of pumpkins ready to be flung into the sheep pasture. (It was only later that I learned sheep have to be taught to recognize pumpkins as food.)

Sheep are very wary about fast-approaching objects, but they don't generally look up when checking for danger. Before we began, I rounded up the sheep and put them in the barn so none would get hit by flying food. Then the pumpkin chucking began.

As it turns out, launching pumpkins into the air is wonderful fun. I have no other redeeming words to say about the event; fun was its sole justification. For hours, pumpkins were launched, until the trebuchet sling wore out. It had been designed for water balloons, not gourds. We still had a pile of pumpkins, so we got the apple-picking ladder and set it out in the field. Everyone took turns climbing the ladder to chuck pumpkins. As some folks threw pumpkins, others ran around the pasture stomping on pumpkin chunks. It was all-around pumpkin mayhem.

We did make a little bit of apple cider on that Apple Day. There was much less than in previous years, but there was just enough for everyone who wanted to get a taste of fresh-pressed juice.

The following spring, despite my fears, the apple trees returned to full bloom. The caterpillars returned too, but not in force. As predicted by experts and doubted by me, the bug population had been significantly diminished by the fact that they had eaten everything the year before and had left virtually nothing for the next generation. What few nests appeared my friends and I cut out of the trees. So the fruit buds survived, and the apples came in such abundance that one tree lost a limb from the weight of them.

I have experienced surprising joy and new life over and over again. They come out of the ground of despair and hopelessness. They ripen and regenerate in such a regular way that you would think I might have come to expect it by now. I have not. I forget the lessons of fall. In the midst of loss, I neglect to notice seeds falling with the power of life in them. Something in that power finds a way.

The year after the tent caterpillars, we had apples again for Apple Day. It was a return of abundance, as if the previous year's scarcity had never happened.

We had something in addition to apples too. A seed from one of the chucked pumpkins had landed outside of the field, where the sheep couldn't reach it. It grew and yielded its own fruit, the fruit of the previous year's pumpkin fun, which was the fruit of an apple failure.

A beautiful orange pumpkin sat on my porch that year, reminding me of other gifts from other seasons. Every year since the caterpillar scourge, the trebuchet has returned, and chucking pumpkins is now a tradition too.

ROSE'S LAST LESSON

I suppose there are as many ways to grieve a dog as there are people and dogs in the world. We who have loved them can describe the exact shape of that dog-sized hole each one leaves in our hearts. Each one we lose is special, and we name each gift they shared to anyone who will ask. We tell each story. We reflect on what they taught us. So it was with the good border collie Rose.

The day Rose died, I had no idea how sick she was. I only knew that as soon as I finished my morning's church work, we were heading to the veterinarian's office. Rose hadn't seemed well for a couple of days. I thought she had some kind of infection. When the vet instead discovered cancer that had attached to Rose's spleen and had shut down her liver, I had to let her go.

The suddenness of this loss left me stunned. Just a few days earlier Rose had been working with me as well as we had ever worked together. Our final lesson had been a joy. We were entered in our third competition together later that month, down in Oregon, and I was thinking we had a good chance at a high score.

Instead, Rose was gone.

Rose was with me for ten months. She came to my farm to be my teacher. The first lesson Rose taught me was the difference between obedience and respect. At mealtimes I have taught my dogs to sit and wait while I measure out their food. When all is ready, I say "OK" and they dive in. But Rose, the highly trained working dog who could take a command on the run from hundreds of yards away, did not "sit." Not once. Because it was my habit with my other dogs, I would often tell her "Sit" as I picked up her bowl at mealtime. She would just stare up at me, as if to say, "Now why on earth would I do that?"

It was not obedience that Rose was interested in. It was partnership. Rose was an outstanding partner. When she saw a reason to lie down, she could drop instantly. When she saw a good reason not to, she would push back on the request and stay on her feet. It was the one thing we fought about. I would ask her for a "Lie down," and she would continue forward.

It was only at the end, before her sudden death, that we came to an understanding. Rose knew what she was doing when she didn't lie down. She knew if she took the "lie down," she would lose her sheep as they bolted away from her. "Lie down" was not the correct command to give. However, Rose had a very useful "Steady," and she would hitch herself and back off.

After Rose's death, many friends reached out to me, as friends do at such times. One of the most comforting things they said was that Rose carried out her teaching job all the way to the end. They were right. Rose taught me what it is like to stand in a competition and trust a dog. Her outwork with me was always spectacular.

Rose was a full-hearted dog who took me more deeply into the lessons of partnership. Whatever kind of sheepdog handler I become, Rose's influence will always be a part of it. She was the first dog to take me to the sheepdog trial "dance," and for that I will always be grateful. Her gift will be reflected in every future run.

A week to the day after Rose died, my young dog Annie gave birth to seven pups. In this circle of life, I was being called again to love what is mortal. Thank you, Rose. Thank you, Annie. Thank you, life.

GETTING TO THANKSGIVING

Living on a farm provides many opportunities for gratitude. Some mornings, simply waking up to the sunrise is enough to inspire me to say, "Thanks." Other times, it's watching my dogs playing with the falling leaves. If morning chores pass without a moment of thanksgiving, then the drive down to the ferry, with a sweeping view of mountains and bay can almost certainly take me there.

Still, there are times when I get up in the dark and do my chores with my head down, so preoccupied with my thoughts that I don't notice the sheep's simple gratitude for the gifts of grain and hay. There are times when the skies are overcast and the drive to the ferry is just another grey commute. Never looking up, I sit in my car with my computer in my lap, answering emails as we cross the water.

When I forget the amazing gift of life, my days usually do not go well. When I forget to begin with gratitude, I can get overwhelmed, making problems bigger than they are or creating problems where there are none. At times like that, it helps me to stop and find a way back to gratitude. Gratitude can usually infuse my mood with deep wonder, and that helps. Gratitude restores my attention to the simple things in each day, the unearned gifts of life. The fresh egg the hen gave me this morning. The woods right outside my window. The good work I am privileged to do, every day. My home. My family. My friends. The breath I am taking right now.

There have been times when gratitude was hard to find. Thanksgiving felt far from me. Many years ago, I went through a season of deep loss, and all I could see was the emptiness of my grief. A friend suggested I make a gratitude list. When she asked, "What do you have in your life that you're grateful for?" I could only list what I didn't have. My friend had to make it simple. "You have a place to live. You ate today. You have people in your life who care."

As hard as it was for me to realize, she was right. So I began to practice gratitude. It wasn't easy, and I wasn't particularly consistent. I didn't always feel grateful. Still, I made gratitude lists. First I could only list a few things. But as I practiced, I noticed more gifts around me. My lists grew longer. These days, my gratitude lists are practically endless.

Of course, a simple "attitude of gratitude" does not make things right. There are moments of deep tragedy. There are times when all one can do is hold on. Storms and fires sweep through communities. Precious people are senselessly murdered in the name of someone's god. We are living on this planet in a way that threatens its future.

But gratitude can be a healing way of moving through tragedy and pain toward hope. Finding something to affirm in the midst of deep grief can be a balm. The psalmists remind us that pouring out the pain in our hearts and leaning into a gracious God can re-center even the most lost soul.

Here in the States, the holiday of Thanksgiving coincides with the end of Ordinary Time. The Sunday after Thanksgiving is usually the first Sunday of Advent. The holiday of gratitude makes way for the season of hope—in contrast to the cultural season of want that kicks off with "Black Friday." To prepare for hope, to resist unnecessary want, I make a list of gratitude, reminding myself that even if I do not get what I want, I will receive what I need.

CONCLUSION
When a Heart Sings

THE RHYTHM OF A SHEPHERD'S YEAR includes times of hard work and times when demands are less intense. Likewise, if one is the pastor of a generous flock, she is granted an occasional sabbatical to rest from the work. The term comes from the Hebrew word for "seven" and points to the basic spiritual idea that every seven days, and every seven years, one should rest. When my sabbatical time came around, I applied for a grant that asked simply, "What would make your heart sing?" When I let that question soak in, the answer was clear. I wanted to go to Great Britain, talk to working shepherds, and watch sheepdog trials. My sabbatical time was refreshing and rich. I did not spend my time visiting exotic places or reading great books or attending profound lectures in prestigious universities. No. I spent my time walking grassy fields or sloshing through mud too deep for any vehicle. I spent it getting up early to join a farmer taking sheep to market; I spent it staying up late to share farm stories with new friends.

Most of all, I spent it watching dogs. In Wales, I spent three days watching as 150 dogs each took a turn at bringing five sheep off a hill 500 yards away. In Ireland, I did the same thing. Another 150 dogs, another 750 sheep, another three days.

Then in Scotland, at the International Trial, it was the top sixty dogs in the British Isles, also faithfully bringing their five sheep home. What I was spending my time watching, over and over again, was the beauty of a dog doing what it was born to do, doing it fully and wholeheartedly, and doing it brilliantly. John Shelby Spong, the Episcopal theologian and bishop, has suggested that this is actually one of the marks of faithful living for those of us who seek to follow Jesus. We are called to "live fully, love wastefully, and be all that God intends us to be."

When, several years later, I returned to the Scottish Isle of Iona, I felt a similar call. Iona is called a "thin place" by many, that is, a place where our physical experience of reality and our awareness of a deeper spiritual reality are so close they can almost touch. In preparation for a trip there with a small flock of congregants, each participant had a special research project and shared the results with the wider group. I knew from my two previous trips to Iona that there are a lot of sheep on the island, of various breeds, so I decided to title my presentation "The Sheep of Iona."

I eagerly gathered information on the different sheep, and I looked through my pictures from previous trips to Iona to find examples. Then I put the information together in a little booklet, printed off twelve copies, and eagerly prepared for an in-depth discussion of various sheep breeds, their characteristics, and their purposes.

The group came together in a circle, waiting to hear from their pastor about their upcoming pilgrimage. I handed out my little booklet and said, "My presentation is on the sheep of Iona." I heard a few snickers. That's when it hit me. Folks had done presentations on the Abbey on Iona, the Nunnery on Iona, Celtic Christianity, the Book of Kells—all thoughtful reflections on spirituality and the nature of pilgrimage.

Now here I was talking about sheep. Not the spirituality of sheep. Actual sheep. What their wool is like. What their ears are like. Different colors of their fleeces. What it means to say this breed is polled, or why this breed is rare, or when shepherding practices changed in the United Kingdom. After I had compared and contrasted three of the six breeds I was featuring, and was only on page two of my booklet, I saw that people's eyes had begun to glaze over. Suddenly I felt like a preacher whose sermon had gone on too long. Using an obscure biblical text. With illustrations that did not relate to anyone's life.

I had become a sheep nerd. By "nerd" I mean someone who gets caught up in a lot of information that the average person doesn't care much about and that probably isn't particularly relevant to most people's lives. One definition includes the observation that a nerd can be "studiously boring."

Preachers can usually tell, as a sermon goes on, when we are just not connecting with the congregation. We see people checking their watches, or discreetly writing notes to their neighbors. But even when we know we are off the rail, we just can't stop ourselves. So I did what many preachers do when they are losing their audience. I began to talk faster. When that didn't seem to help, I started cutting here and there, leaving unsaid my brilliant observations about this particular breed or that particular type. When I got to the Bluefaced Leicester, though, I couldn't resist. I just had to tell the group about the Border Leicester too, cousin to the Bluefaced, and star of the movie "Babe."

I heard myself explaining that the Texel makes a nice foundation ewe. "Stop!" some part of me was pleading. But I had to tell our group about the Hebridian, a primitive breed with fantastical horns. "The ubiquitous Scottie ewe also has horns." I had to add. "The distinctive looking Zwartble is naturally polled—no horns on the ewes or the rams. My breed, the Romney, is not found on Iona."

When I finally finished talking, the group sat in stunned silence. Then we moved on. Inside, I laughed at myself. Yes, I am a sheep nerd.

I agree with the words of the conservationist John Muir, who was instrumental in the establishment of our country's national park system 150 years ago. "When we try to pick out anything by itself, we find it hitched to everything else in the Universe." God is found not only in the places we call sacred, but in the very specific details of the obscure. It's all hitched, and any deep exploration of the sacred or the mundane leads us to the same place. I believe any deep exploration of the details of one's life will lead us deeper into spirituality itself. Throughout my year, and everywhere on the farm and in my congregation, I see God.

ACKNOWLEDGMENTS

No matter the flock she is tending, a shepherd knows she cannot do her work alone. I am deeply grateful for all who have supported my work and encouraged my words.

Thank you to all the folks at University Congregational United Church of Christ, for all the ways they have allowed me to shepherd them these last two decades.

Thank you to my sabbatical team of Mary, Kathryn, Debra, and Sally, who walked me through this writing and editing process and cheered me every step of the way.
who took my stories and made them flow.

Thank you to those who taught me about sheep and sheepdogs and about living on a farm. Please note that my observations are meant to be about life and should not be taken as sheep-raising advice. For that I would refer you to the experts.

Thank you to Lori and her daughters Kelly and Nikki, who have helped ewes in trouble, rounded up wayward rams, and carried newborn lambs to the barn when I have been away from the farm.

And especially, thank you to my family, who listens to my stories and asks me for more. Here you go.